EXPLORATORY PROBLEMS IN MATHEMATICS

by

Frederick W. Stevenson
University of Arizona

National Council of Teachers of Mathematics

Copyright © 1992 by
THE NATIONAL COUNCIL OF TEACHERS OF MATHEMATICS, INC.
1906 Association Drive, Reston, Virginia 22091
All rights reserved

Library of Congress Cataloging-in-Publication Data:

Stevenson, Frederick W.
   Exploratory problems in mathematics / by Frederick W. Stevenson.
      p.   cm.
   Includes bibliographical references.
   ISBN 0-87353-338-0
   1. Mathematics—Problems, exercises, etc.   I. Title.
QA43.S793   1991
510'.76—dc20   91-34782
                                                                                    CIP

Printed in the United States of America

CONTENTS

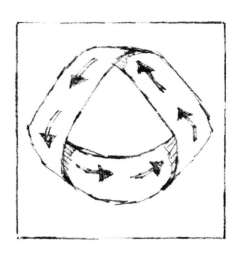

PREFACE

It was not until my fourteenth year of mathematics courses that I was introduced to open-ended problems. During my second year in graduate school at the University of Colorado, Wolfgang Thron taught a topology course that had accessible problems without accessible solutions. It was the first time in my life that I was challenged to express myself mathematically. It was so exciting that I did my thesis work in topology. Yet when I began teaching, I forgot entirely about open-ended problems. I taught in the same style that I had been taught—"For homework, do the first ten problems; the answers to the odd-numbered ones are in the back of the book." Ten years later, when I spent a sabbatical semester in Israel, I became reacquainted with open-ended problems. Shmuel Avital of the Technion University was creating these kinds of problems for precollege students.

For the past twelve years, I have been searching for open-ended problems that can be used to introduce students to the creative side of mathematics. I began with a list of eight problems that I used in a summer institute for high school teachers. The list grew to twelve for the following year and then to fifteen. It now stands at sixty. These problems are called *exploratory problems* to conform to the common parlance of the day. They range in accessibility from grade school to graduate school, and they have been used in a variety of settings: institutes for schoolteachers, camps for gifted junior high school students, classes at the University of Arizona, and independent projects for graduate students.

The problems are formulated somewhat differently from those open-ended problems in my topology class. Instead of opening with the classic question, "What can you say about . . .?," I have built the problems around specific numbers so that specific answers can be found. However, I have tried to make the numbers so big that there is ample room for proper mathematical exploration. The computer can sometimes meet the challenge before the mind gets sufficient exercise, and in those instances, I recommend that higher numbers be used.

Until now, I have resisted pleas to write a book. Ideally, I like to pose a question and hang around to help out. I was convinced that it was an impossible task to properly supply helpful hints in print. In the first place, hints must be tailored to the individual student. They must take into account different backgrounds, different mindsets, and different personalities. There are some people who don't want any help at all; there are others who want help right away. Secondly, hints must be offered at the right time, and that depends entirely on the progress of the exploration. This can only be determined by being present during the course of the investigation. Nevertheless, it is important to reach all those students and teachers who want to try their hand at creative mathematics but don't know where to start. So here is the attempt. If the hints seem sparse, you will understand why. If you need help and have nowhere to turn, you may write to me. Also, if you find an especially pleasing solution that you want to share, feel free to write. Nothing beats an elegant solution in mathematics.

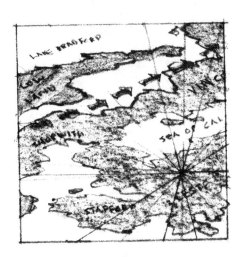

INTRODUCTION

THE two core courses in the school curriculum are mathematics and English. Both are taught every semester for all, or nearly all, the first twelve years of school. Both cover basic skills that are necessary to function in the adult world. Both can be deadly dull for students. Mathematics consists of systems of rules, arbitrary notation, facts to be memorized, and repetitive homework assignments. English consists of vocabulary, parts of speech, grammar, and sentence structure. But there is a difference. Whereas mathematics courses hone the skills of the students and make them competent, English classes introduce students to the world of literature. While learning English, students read the works of the great creative minds. Furthermore, they are encouraged to create their own individual world and write about it.

The word *creative* in mathematics is, more often than not, a synonym for *wrong*. After all, the student believes, the world of mathematics has already been created. It already has its algorithms and formulas. There appears to be no place for new ideas, or, at least, no chance that any average student would have a worthwhile new idea. Creativity in mathematics surely is reserved for geniuses like Isaac Newton.

Fortunately, this is not a fair description of the world of mathematics. Mathematics *is* as creative as the arts. Furthermore, this creative aspect can be shared by grade school, junior high school, and high school students. It is not the private domain of geniuses or of Ph.D.'s. This book is an attempt to inspire such creativity.

The problems in the book are called *exploratory problems*. Doing such problems can be likened to a trek into the wilderness. There is uncertainty, frustration, and fatigue; there is also excitement, beauty, and the thrill of discovery. There should be no rush or sense of urgency to "get it over with." There is no grade waiting at the end of the exploration.

Good mathematical problems are not in short supply. They are in books and in magazines; they are communicated at conventions, by computer

1

lines, and by the grapevine. I have chosen some that satisfy my own special criteria, as follows:

- The problem should be immediately attractive.
- The problem should be approached by gathering or generating data.
- The problem should offer something interesting at many levels, from junior high school to graduate school.
- The concepts involved must be fundamental to mathematics.
- The solution to the problem should be satisfying.
- The problem should suggest several other problems.

These criteria exclude certain types of problems—the complicated or technical problems, the brain teasers and logical paradoxes, the single or short answer problems, and, unfortunately, many clever problems in geometry. What I have included are problems that, I hope, will entertain, entrap, and enlighten. If all goes well, these questions will suggest other questions, and before long, the students will be formulating and investigating ideas of their own. This is creativity in mathematics.

There are sixty problems in the book. Each is placed in one of three categories: excursions, expeditions, or computer-assisted explorations. The excursions are generally shorter and perhaps easier; the expeditions are more extensive and open ended; the computer explorations need a programmable hand calculator or a computer. The categories are somewhat arbitrary, and the placement of the problems is as well. Since the distinction between categories is fuzzy anyway, we placed twenty problems in each category for the sake of symmetry. It is especially difficult to confine the category of computer-assisted explorations to twenty problems. The computer is becoming so familiar to students nowadays that they can use its power effectively in many different contexts. Nevertheless, I believe that at least half the problems here can still best be approached by the time-honored method of pencil and paper.

These problems are meant to be played with over a period of time. They are strictly for intellectual enjoyment and excitement. There is no solution manual; there is no book of hints. The philosophy of the book is that the freedom of inquiry and the thrill of discovery are of foremost importance. Hints or readily available answers might compromise this. I will say that several explorations involve such famous fascinations as prime numbers, Fibonacci sequences, Pascal's triangle, continued fractions, and, yes, even chaos.

1

THE EXPLORATORY PROCESS

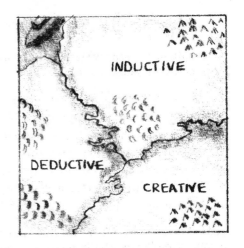

We shall divide the exploratory process into three parts: the inductive, the deductive, and the creative. Roughly speaking, this means that (1) we search for the answer, (2) after finding the answer, we try to understand why it works, and (3) we initiate our own explorations. Although this explanation may not capture exactly what goes on, we have tried to adopt problems for the book that fit this model.

The search begins with gathering data. Actually, generating data may be more accurate. Data are the raw material of our exploration and may be generated by hand, by calculator, or by computer. In most problems, the computer is not needed, but it can be very helpful.

After the data have been generated, they must be organized. The organizational scheme releases the patterns and relationships that are hidden in the raw data. Usually, a variety of schemes will work. The one that we choose is important because it will directly influence the course of the search.

Once a pattern that fits the data has been discovered, it must be tested against more data. If the pattern endures, then the answer should be close at hand. The problems in the book are posed with specific numbers, and usually the pattern can be pushed far enough to reach the numbers.

Finding the answer completes the inductive phase of the exploration, and for some, it marks the end of the problem.

Although finding the answer is surely the immediate goal, there is a longer-range goal—to understand what is really going on in the problem. This is a rather vague goal, and it will be approached in different ways by different people.

One question that might begin this inquiry is this: If we change the specific numbers in the problem to general numbers, can we extend and generalize the patterns that we discovered? If we can, it usually means we have discovered a formula and that we have developed a deeper understanding of the problem than was required by simple pattern recognition.

3

Another leading question is this: What is the mathematical context that has produced these patterns? This question is especially vague and open ended, but it is at the heart of the problem. If we can answer this question, we will be on the way to finishing the deductive phase of the exploration.

Completing the deductive phase of the exploration is a long-range goal indeed. It may take months or even years, but keep in mind that there is no hurry; there is no time limit on these problems.

The last part of the exploratory process is called *creative*. Creativity plays a part in the inductive and the deductive phases of the process, but we use the word here in a particular way. During the exploration, there may have been some tangential items that attracted our attention. Putting these items into a mathematical context, that is, defining the terms, setting the parameters, formulating the questions, and then pursuing the answers, is our version of the creative aspect of the exploration.

This part of the exploratory process is never finished. This is the essence of mathematical research.

In this chapter and in chapter 2 we give examples of short explorations to give a flavor of what the process is like. Chapters 3, 4, and 5 are devoted to full-length explorations.

THE QUESTION

Pick any two positive integers (they can be the same number), add them, multiply them, and then add the resulting sum and product together. What is the largest number less than 50 that you can *not* get with this process?

Inductive Phase

We shall split the inductive parts into six steps.

Step 1. Generate data.

For this problem, let us start with several examples. If we pick 3 and 5, then $3 + 5 = 8$, $3 \times 5 = 15$, and $8 + 15 = 23$. If we pick 1 and 2, then $1 + 2 = 3$, $1 \times 2 = 2$, and $3 + 2 = 5$. If we pick 7 and 4, then $7 + 4 = 11$, $7 \times 4 = 28$, and $11 + 28 = 39$.

Step 2. Organize data.

Generally it is best to start with small numbers and work your way up. It is also a good idea to keep track of your findings in a table (see table 1.1).

Step 3. Look for patterns.

We can see from the chart that if one of the numbers is 1, then we get answers of the form 3, 5, 7—in fact, all the odd numbers except 1. We can write these numbers as $1 + 2k$, where $k = 1, 2, 3, \ldots$. If 2 is one of the

Table 1.1
Organizing data

Numbers	Sum	Product	Combined Sum
1, 1	2	1	3
1, 2	3	2	5
1, 3	4	3	7
1, 4	5	4	9
1, 5	6	5	11
.			
.			
.			
2, 1	3	2	5
2, 2	4	4	8
2, 3	5	6	11
2, 4	6	8	14
2, 5	7	10	17
.			
.			
.			
3, 1	4	3	7
3, 2	5	6	11
3, 3	6	9	15
3, 4	7	12	19
3, 5	8	15	23
.			
.			
.			

numbers, we get answers of the form 5, 8, 11, 14, . . .; that is, numbers of the form $2 + 3k$, where $k = 1, 2, 3, ...$ If 3 is one of the numbers, then we get, as answers, numbers of the form $3 + 4k$. Presumably, if we extend the table using 4, we would get answers of the form $4 + 5k$. We should check this.

Step 4. Generate more data.

In order to corroborate our suspicions, let us gather more data.

Numbers	Sum	Product	Combined Sum
4, 1	5	4	9
4, 2	6	8	14
4, 3	7	12	19
4, 4	8	16	24
4, 5	9	20	29

Yes, these answers are of the form $4 + 5k$.

Step 5. Fit formulas to patterns.

The formula that might work here is this: if m is one of the numbers, then our answers will be of the form $m + (m+1)k$, where $k = 1, 2, 3,$ . . . . We can also see that if the other number we choose is n, then we get $m + (m + 1)n$. Actually, we can figure this formula out from algebra.

Given m and n—if we add them, $m + n$; multiply them, mn; and then add their sum and product, $m + n + mn$, we do get $m + (m+1)n$.

Step 6. Answer the question.

Our original question was to find numbers that cannot appear as answers in our list. Let us write down the first 49 numbers and cross out those that do appear. Here are the first 30:

1   2   ̶3̶   4   ̶5̶   6   ̶7̶   ̶8̶   ̶9̶   10

̶1̶1̶   12   ̶1̶3̶   ̶1̶4̶   ̶1̶5̶   16   ̶1̶7̶   18   ̶1̶9̶   ̶2̶0̶

̶2̶1̶   22   ̶2̶3̶   ̶2̶4̶   ̶2̶5̶   ̶2̶6̶   ̶2̶7̶   28   ̶2̶9̶   30

Notice that we have crossed out the numbers every time they appear; so some numbers have been crossed out many times. The important thing, however, is to find the numbers that remain uncrossed. In this chart, the largest such number is 30 itself. If you extend this to 49, and you should, you will find that 46 is the largest uncrossed-out number. Therefore, 46 is the answer to our question.

The question has been answered, and this will be enough for some. Others might want to pursue the problem further.

Deductive Phase

Although we did find an answer, what is going on behind the patterns may still remain a mystery. The process of crossing out numbers is reminiscent of the sieve of Eratosthenes. Since the sieve is a method used to find prime numbers, the resemblance suggests that the numbers we locate here may be relatives of primes. And so they are. The numbers not crossed out in our list are the numbers that are one less than prime numbers. That is curious. Why is it that the numbers produced by adding, multiplying, and then adding the results are all numbers that are one less than a composite number? Mathematically, the question is, Why is a number of the form $m + (m+1)n$ also of the form $ab - 1$, where a and $b > 1$?

Algebra provides the answer.

$$m + (m+1)n + 1 = (m+1) + (m+1)n = (m+1)(n+1) = ab,$$

where $a, b > 1$.

So $m + (m+1)n = ab - 1$.

Creative Phase

While doing this problem, other questions may have crossed our minds. For example, what happens if we insist that our two original numbers be different?

Question. Choose two *different* positive numbers. Add them, multiply them, then add the sum and product. What is the largest number less than 50 that you cannot get this way?

Another question might be, What happens if we subtract instead of add?

Question. Choose two positive numbers. Subtract the smaller from the larger. Multiply them. Add the difference and the product. What is the largest number less than 50 you cannot get this way?

Question. Given two positive numbers, add them, multiply them, and subtract the smaller from the larger. What is the largest number less than 50 that you cannot get?

While crossing out the numbers between 1 and 49 that you do obtain, you may wonder which number or numbers have been crossed out the most times.

Question. Which of the numbers less than 50 can be obtained in the greatest number of ways using the process of adding, multiplying, and adding the results?

These four questions, like any that spring to mind during an exploration, are uneven in value. Some may be good, some may be silly on further investigation, some are straightforward, and some are too hard. You won't know until you have tried them. The most important thing is to ask questions. When you do this, you are creating mathematics that is yours.

2

EXPLORING
WITH A
CALCULATOR

The hand calculator is now a part of every mathematics student's school supplies, just as a pencil and paper were in the past (and still are). In this chapter, we will incorporate the calculator into an exploration. In nearly every problem in the book, the calculator can help, if only as an aid in computing. In some problems, it can be used in a creative way, and in some it is nearly indispensable. In this question, we will use a simple hand calculator both as a computing tool and as a creative tool. Then we will use a programmable hand calculator to finish the problem. We will follow the same investigative format as in chapter 1.

THE QUESTION

Which unit fraction $1/n$, for $n \le 50$, has the decimal expansion of longest period?

Inductive Phase

Step 1. Generate data.

We shall list the decimal expansions of the first nine unit fractions. These can be figured by hand or with a simple calculator. All that is required is division.

$1/2 = 0.5$	$1/7 = 0.\overline{142857}$
$1/3 = 0.\overline{3}$	$1/8 = 0.125$
$1/4 = 0.25$	$1/9 = 0.\overline{1}$
$1/5 = 0.2$	$1/10 = 0.1$
$1/6 = 0.1\overline{6}$	

The bar over the numbers means that the pattern repeats. The calculator might not convince you of the repetition of 1/7, but working with pencil and paper and long division will convince you.

Step 2. Organize data.

Let us put the data into a chart that distinguishes the different behaviors of the decimal expansions.

Terminating	Repeating	Repeating after delay
1/2	1/3	1/6
1/4	1/7	
1/5	1/9	
1/8		
1/10		

Step 3. Look for patterns.

The column of terminating decimals contains most of the entries. They all have even denominators except 1/5. The column of repeating decimals contains fractions with odd denominators. The column with decimals that repeat after delay has a single entry, 1/6. There isn't much information to go on here.

Step 4. Generate more data.

Let us use a simple calculator now. It displays eight digits and a decimal. Sometimes it gives a clear indication of the right answer. Sometimes it gives numbers that may or may not repeat—these are indicated with a question mark in the following list:

$1/11 = 0.0\overline{9}$ $1/12 = 0.08\overline{3}$ $1/13 = 0.076\ 923$?
$1/14 = 0.071\ 428\ 5$? $1/15 = 0.0\overline{6}$ $1/16 = 0.062\ 5$
$1/17 = 0.058\ 823\ 5$? $1/18 = 0.0\overline{5}$ $1/19 = 0.052\ 631\ 5$?
$1/20 = 0.05$ $1/21 = 0.0476\ 19$? $1/22 = 0.0\overline{45}$
$1/23 = 0.043\ 478\ 1$? $1/24 = 0.041\ \overline{6}$ $1/25 = 0.04$

Placing these data into our chart, we get the following:

Terminating	Repeating	Repeating after delay
1/16	1/11	1/12
1/20	1/13 ?	1/14 ?
1/25	1/17 ?	1/15
	1/19 ?	1/18
	1/21 ?	1/22
	1/23 ?	1/24

Step 5. Fit formulas to patterns.

Combining these data with the data of step 2, we begin to see some patterns. In the column of terminating decimals, the denominators of the fractions are 2, 4, 5, 8, 10, 16, 20, and 25. Every one of these numbers has the property that either 2 divides it, or 5 divides it, or both 2 and 5 divide it. No other prime divides any of these numbers. In the column of decimals that repeat after delay, the denominators of the fractions are 6, 12, 14(?), 15, 18, 22, and 24. Every one of these numbers is divisible by 2 and a prime other than 2 or 5, or by 5 and a prime other than 2 or 5. In the column of repeating decimals, the denominators are 3, 7, 9, 11, 13(?), 17(?), 19(?), 21(?), and 23(?). Although five of these numbers are placed in this column by guesswork, it appears as if the fractions that repeat have denominators that are odd and have no factor of 5.

If our original question for $1/n$ were for $n \leq 25$, then we could simply check out the candidates 1/13, 1/17, 1/19, 1/21, and 1/23 by hand and be done with it. But we must go to 50. That is a lot of work for pencil and paper, although if we were to try it, we would soon become creative to save time. And a lot of time can be saved because many curious shortcuts can be found. But a calculator is quicker, and it can be used creatively, too.

First we will use a simple calculator, later a programmable calculator.

Let us look at 1/17. Our calculator tells us the decimal expansion is 0.058 823 5. To find the next digit in the decimal expansion after 5, we multiply by 10.

$$10 \,(1/17) = 10/17 = 0.588\ 235\ 2.$$

So 1/17 = 0.058 823 52. The numeral 2 is the next digit. Let us try for the next digit.

$$10 \,(10/17) = 100/17 = 5.882\ 352\ 9$$

So 1/17 = 0.058 823 529. Numeral 9 is the next digit. Multiplying once more by 10 gives us 1000/17 = 58.823 529. This time we do not get the next digit. But we can do something. Notice that 1000/17 = 58 + 14/17. You can figure this out by hand, or if you wish, you may use the calculator. Simply mimic what you did by hand, multiply 17 by 58, and subtract the product from 1000:

$$17 \times 58 = 986$$
$$1000 - 986 = 14$$

Now 14/17 = 0.823 529 4. Behold, we have our next digit—it is 4. So, at this stage, we know that 1/17 = 0.058 823 529 4. There is no sign of repetition yet.

We can do this process of extending the known decimal much more efficiently. Since our calculator gives us eight digits, we can find several new digits at a time rather than just one new one. Let us do our procedure again but multiply by 1 000 000:

$$1/17 = 0.058\ 823\ 5$$
$$\text{so } 1\ 000\ 000/17 = 58\ 823.529$$
$$= 58\ 823 + 9/17$$

Now

$$9/17 = 0.529\ 411\ 7$$
$$\text{so } 1\ 000\ 000/17 = 58\ 823.529\ 411\ 7.$$

Therefore $1/17 = 0.058\ 823\ 529\ 411\ 7$.

This demonstration increased our known digits by six, but there is still no sign of repetition. Let us try it again. This time we will work on 9/17.

$$1\ 000\ 000\ (9/17) = 529\ 411.76$$
$$= 529\ 411 + 13/17$$
$$\text{Since } 13/17 = 0.764\ 705\ 8,$$
$$9/17 = 0.529\ 411\ 764\ 705\ 8.$$

Now we have $1/17 = 0.058\ 823\ 529\ 411\ 764\ 705\ 8$. It seems we have repetition! The 058 at the end of the number is like the beginning. This is not a 100 percent guarantee, but we'll take it. The pattern is sixteen digits long.

Let us try 1/19:

$$1/19 = 0.052\ 631\ 5;$$
$$1\ 000\ 000/19 = 52\ 621.578 = 52\ 631 + 11/19$$
$$11/19 = 0.578\ 947\ 3;$$
$$11\ 000\ 000/19 = 578\ 947.36 = 578\ 947 + 7/19$$
$$7/19 = 0.368\ 421;$$
$$7\ 000\ 000/19 = 368\ 421.05 = 368\ 421 + 1/19$$

We know 1/19 already. So $1/19 = 0.\overline{052\ 631\ \underline{578\ 947}\ \underline{368\ 421}}$. The underlined numerals show where our procedure overlaps answers. We can see that 1/19 has a repetitive decimal expansion of period 18—a new record.

Let us try 1/21:

$$1/21 = 0.047\ 619;$$
$$1\ 000\ 000/21 = 47\ 619.047 = 47\ 619 + 1/21$$

Our answer is $1/21 = 0.\overline{047\ 619}$, a pattern of length 6.

Our last fraction to try is 1/23:

$$1/23 = 0.043\ 478\ 2;$$
$$1\ 000\ 000/23 = 43\ 478.26 = 43\ 478 + 6/23$$
$$6/23 = 0.260\ 869\ 5;$$
$$6\ 000\ 000/23 = 260\ 869.56 = 260\ 869 + 13/23$$

$$13/23 = 0.565\ 217\ 3;$$
$$13\ 000\ 000/23 = 565\ 217.39 = 565\ 217 + 9/23$$
$$9/23 = 0.391\ 304\ 3;$$
$$9\ 000\ 000/23 = 391\ 304.34 = 391\ 304 + 8/23$$
$$8/23 = 0.347\ 826.$$

Whew! Let us stop and put it together:

$$1/23 = 0.043\ 478\ \underline{2}60\ 869\ \underline{5}65\ 217\ 391\ 304\ \underline{3}47\ 826$$

Wait—the 043 478 26 at the end is a repetition. So our answer is

$$1/23 = 0.\overline{043\ 478\ 260\ 869\ 565\ 217\ 391\ 3},$$

a period of length 22!

It would be nice if we could find a way to generate the fractions 1/23, 6/23, 13/23, 9/23, 8/23 without all this multiplying by 1 000 000 and then dividing. How are the numerators 1, 6, 13, 9, and 8 related for denominator 23? The answer probably lies in the same place as the answer to the questions "How are 1, 9, and 13 related for denominator 17?" and "How are 1, 11, and 7 related for denominator 19?" If we could answer these, the time needed to find the answer to the first question would be shorter.

We have yet to see a convincing pattern that will lead us to the answer. The chart below summarizes what we know:

Denominator	Length of pattern
3	1
7	6
11	2
13	6
17	16
19	18
23	22

It appears that the lengths are less than the denominators, and the best we can hope for is that the length is one less. This seems to occur only for prime numbers, and even then it does not always happen. As of now, it appears that the best hope for the longest repeating pattern is 47. If we are lucky, the length of the pattern for 1/47 will be 46.

Step 6. Answer the question.

Although we could proceed by hand or by calculator, let us finish the problem quickly with a programmable hand calculator.

We are using a Tandy PC 6, but others are equally as good. The following program is in BASIC, and it mimics the way we find decimal expansions using pencil and paper:

```
10  INPUT "NUM", N
20  INPUT "DEN", D
30  A = N
40  B = A * 10
50  C = INT (B/D)
60  PRINT C
70  E = B − C*D
80  IF E = N THEN GOTO 110
90  A = E
100 GOTO 40
110 END
```
(Or GOTO 10 if you wish to find another expansion.)

Using this program, you will generate another digit in the decimal expansion on the screen every time you push the EXE (execute key) until one full period is finished.

For example, for NUM = 1, DEN = 29 you will get

$$1/29 = 0.\overline{034\ 482\ 758\ 620\ 689\ 655\ 172\ 413\ 793\ 1},$$

a record length of 28!

If you get tired of pushing EXE to spin out the decimal expansion, you may adapt the program like this to read out only the length of the pattern:

Add:
```
25  I = 0
105 PRINT I
```

Change:
```
60  I = I + 1 (this replaces PRINT C )
80  change "110" to "105"
```

Using this program, we can finish our chart out to 50 (or beyond, if we wish):

Denominator	Length of pattern
27	3
29	28
31	15
33	2
37	3
39	6
41	5
43	21
47	46
49	42

We have our answer, and it was what we expected—1/47 has the decimal expansion with the longest pattern. Its pattern has length 46.

Deductive Phase

We have made several observations during this investigation. For example, the behavior of the decimal expansion of $1/n$ depends on the factors of n, specifically, the factors 2 and 5.

1. Decimal expansions of $1/n$ terminate if n is the product of only 2s, 5s, or 2s and 5s.

2. The expansion delays and then repeats if n has a factor of 2 and/or 5 as well as other factors.

3. The expansion repeats without delay if n has no 2s or 5s as factors.

We have also noticed curiosities about the period of a repeating expansion:

4. The period of a repeating decimal expansion for $1/n$ is always $< n$.

5. The period may be as large as $n - 1$ and often is, if n is a prime number. If n is composite, the period seems to be considerably shorter.

6. If n is a prime and the period of its expansion is not $n - 1$, it seems to be a factor of $n - 1$.

Some of these observations can be validated.

Presumably, if a decimal expansion terminates, there will be a term after which all succeeding terms are 0. We have already used a hand calculator to find the succeeding terms of an expansion. We simply multiply the numerator by more and more 10s. Apparently, if we multiply $1/n$ by enough 10s, we get a whole number (followed by all 0s). In fact, this is what happens.

Suppose n has only factors of 2s, 5s, or 2s and 5s. So $n = 2^a 5^b$. Now $10^k/n = I$, a whole number, if $k =$ the larger of a and b.

To make this real, let us look at an example, say 1/40. Now $40 = 2^3 5$. So $10^3/40$ should be an integer, and it is, 25. So $1/40 = 0.025$, a decimal that terminates after three places. This discussion leads to a theorem:

THEOREM. *The fraction $1/n$ terminates after k places if n is a product of powers of 2 and/or 5 and k is the higher power of the factor of 2 or 5.*

Decimal expansions that delay before repeating can be approached with the same reasoning. If there is a delay of length k, then presumably $10^k/n$ will produce an integer followed by a repeating expansion. In fact, if $n = 2^a 5^b m$, then $10^k/n = d/m$, where k is the larger of a and b, and $d = 10^k/2^a 5^b$. Now $d/m = I + r/m$ where I is the quotient and r the remainder in the division process.

Let us look at an example to bring reality to this general discussion. Consider 1/240, which equals $0.004\overline{16}$. The delay is of length 4. If we multiply 1/240 by 10 000, we should get an integer followed by a repeating decimal, and of course, we do—10 000/240 = $41.\overline{6}$. Notice that 240 = $2^4 \times 5 \times 3$; so 4 is the higher power of a factor 2 or 5 in the number 240. Since 1000/240 = 41 + 2/3, our analysis above seems legitimate.

THEOREM. *The fraction $1/n$ will delay k places and then repeat like r/m for an $r < m$, where k is the higher power of the factors of 2 or 5 that divide n and m is the number you get by factoring the 2s and 5s out of n.*

The question still remains whether fractions $1/n$ actually do repeat if n is devoid of the factors of 2 and 5.

Let us examine this question with the help of the example in figure 2.1 using long division.

```
        0.  1 4 2 8 5 7
    7 ) 1. 0 0 0 0 0 0
        7
        3 0
        2 8
          2 0
          1 4
            6 0
            5 6
              4 0
              3 5
                5 0
                4 9
                  1
```

Fig. 2.1

Notice that at each step, we divide 7 into a power of 10 and get a new remainder. The remainders in this example are, successively 1, 3, 2, 6, 4, 5, and 1 again. Once we reach a remainder that we have already obtained, the expansion begins a repetitive cycle. If we first reach the remainder 1, then the expansion repeats its front end. That was the situation with 1/7. But until we reach a familiar remainder, the expansion will continue to grow, one new remainder at a time, without repetition. There are at most six possible different remainders when 7 is the denominator (0 is not possible because the expansion does not terminate). Therefore, the period can be at most 6. In general, the period of $1/n$ can be at most $n-1$.

THEOREM. *If $1/n$ has a periodic expansion, the period is less than n.*

But the question of repetition is still unresolved. Does $1/n$ have a periodic expansion? Might it not happen that when we are finding remainders, the number 1 never occurs again because another remainder has occurred twice in the meantime, thus creating a cycle excluding 1?

In other words, could we have the situation in figure 2.2 in the long division process? Let the first a be the jth remainder; the second a, the kth remainder. We assume that the remainder 1 does not occur before j or between j and k.

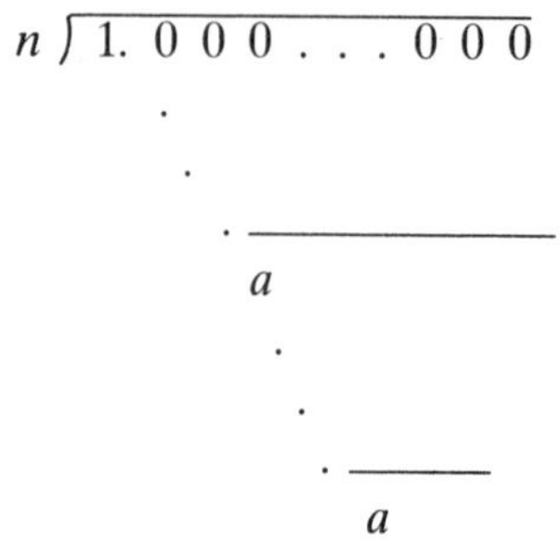

$$n \overline{) \, 1. \, 0 \, 0 \, 0 \, . \, . \, . \, 0 \, 0 \, 0}$$

.

.

$\overline{\qquad\qquad}$

a

.

.

.

$\overline{\qquad}$

a

Fig. 2.2

First we have $10^j/n = I + a/n$ and $10^k/n = I' + a/n$ where I and I' are integers. So

$$10^k/n - 10^j/n = 10^j(10^i - 1)/n = I' - I,$$

where $i = k - j$. Since n does not divide 10^j (because n is devoid of 2s and 5s), it follows that n divides $10^i - 1$. Therefore, $(10^i - 1)/n = I''$ (an integer), so $10^i/n = I'' + 1/n$. Thus 1 repeats at the ith place. But $i < k$, and this goes against our supposition. This shows that 1 is a remainder that will occur again, and it is the first such remainder to do so. Therefore a cycle of repetition will be formed, and the expansion will be periodic.

THEOREM. *The fraction $1/n$ will repeat without delay if n has no factors of 2 or 5.*

We have not, by any means, exhausted the theory behind decimal expansions. A course in number theory will provide further insight.

Creative Phase

There are several areas that would be fun to investigate further. Here are three:

1. Size of periods

If the decimal expansion of $1/n$ is periodic, what is the period if—

    a) n is the product of two primes? Of three primes?

    b) n is the square of a prime? The cube of a prime?

2. Numbers in the decimal expansion

   a) Suppose you remove the decimal from the front of the expansion of 1/7 and remove the bar from the top. You get 142 857. What do you get if you multiply this number by 2? By 3? By 4? . . .?

   b) Perform the same trick on the expansion of 1/13. Is the same thing happening as in 2a? Repeat this for 1/17 and for 1/19.

   c) The expansion of 1/7 has period 6, an even number. Compare the numbers in the first half of the period, 1, 4, 2, to the numbers in the last half, 8, 5, 7. Do you notice anything? Make this comparison between the first and second halves of periods for other expansions of even period. What do you notice?

   d) Suppose that the expansion of 1/*n* has a period divisible by 3. Can you say anything about the numbers in the first third of the period compared to the second third and the last third?

3. Remainders

   a) We have seen the successive remainders when 1/7 is worked out by long division. They are 1, 3, 2, 6, 4, 5, and 1 again. Can you get these without doing the long division? Perhaps if you look at every second remainder it will help.

   b) Look at the successive remainders you get for 1/13, 1/17, and 1/19 and figure out an easy way of finding them.

   c) While doing step 5 of the inductive phase with the hand calculator, we found ourselves wondering about a shortcut to finding every sixth remainder of the division process for 1/17, and 1/19, and 1/23. What is the shortcut?

Lots of other explorations will suggest themselves as you do these. In fact, this area of investigation is so fertile that we have two problems in chapter 8 devoted to it: "Periodic Fractions" and "The Universe of Fractions with a Prime Denominator."

3

A MATHEMATICAL EXCURSION

The problems in this book are all presented in the same format. The title is followed by a paragraph about the problem. Next come "The Questions" and finally, a section called "A Beginning," which gives the student a start on the problem. The title is usually meant to be clever and is supposed to catch the student's eye. The paragraph that follows puts the problem into perspective. The questions are usually in order of difficulty or complexity. "A Beginning" answers the questions in simplified form. This not only helps the student get started but is also supposed to remove any doubts about how to interpret the questions.

In this chapter, we give an example of an excursion, complete with different methods of investigation. This example shows the power of the computer or the programmable hand calculator and introduces two techniques for building formulas to fit patterns.

Building Pyramids out of Tennis Balls

You have just finished your tennis lesson and are gathering up the balls. Suppose that you were to stack up all the balls in the shape of a pyramid. I wonder how high it would be? Hmmmm.

THE QUESTIONS

Suppose that you have 1000 tennis balls. You want to build the largest triangular pyramid that you can.

1. How many balls are in your pyramid?

2. How many levels high is the pyramid?

3. How many more balls would you need to build a pyramid with one more level?

A BEGINNING

Suppose that you have only twelve balls. Figure 3.1 shows a pyramid with two levels made up of four balls; figure 3.2 shows a three-level pyramid made up of ten balls. This pyramid would be the largest you could form with twelve balls. You would have two balls left over. The next larger pyramid would need a fourth level of balls. Since each level seems to be made up of a triangular array of balls, we can figure out how many balls should be in the bottom level of a four-level pyramid.

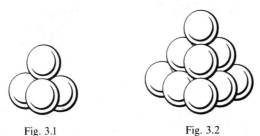

Fig. 3.1   Fig. 3.2

The first level is one ball; the second level, three balls; the third level, six balls; the fourth level, ten balls.

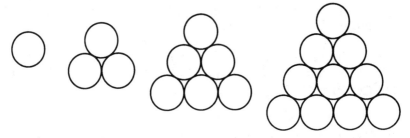

So a four-level pyramid contains twenty balls. We need eight more than we have.

You might want to take some time and try the problem yourself before reading further. As in the previous investigations we shall carry out our explanation in three phases: the inductive, the deductive, and the creative.

THE EXPLORATION

Inductive Phase

In pursuing this problem, we can build more and more levels for the foundation and simply count the balls as in the chart in figure 3.3. We can continue this chart by hand until we reach 1000 balls in the right-hand column (labeled P). There is a nice pattern here. We can form the next level in column T by adding the next number in column N, 6, to the last

Number of levels N	Number of balls in a level T	Number of balls in the pyramid P
1	1	1
2	3	4
3	6	10
4	10	20
5	15	35

Fig. 3.3

number in column T, 15. We can denote that like this:

$$T(6) = 6 + T(5) = 6 + 15 = 21$$

And using similar notation, we find the total number of balls in the pyramid, $P(6)$, to be $T(6) + P(5) = 56$. If $N = 7$, we get $T(7) = 7 + T(6) = 28$; $P(7) = T(7) + P(6) = 28 + 56 = 84$.

This sort of pattern is tailor-made for the computer or programmable hand calculator. Using BASIC on our Tandy PC 6, we wrote a program that will produce as many entries as you wish.

```
10 N = 1          (N represents the number of the level.)
20 T = 1          (T is the number of balls in the level.)
30 P = 1          (P is the number of balls in the pyramid.)
40 PRINT N; T; P
50 N = N+1        (Add 1 to the level.)
60 T = T+N        (Add balls to make a new foundation.)
70 P = P+T        (Total the balls in the new pyramid.)
80 GOTO 40        (Print the entries and repeat the process.)
```

Every time you push the EXE (execute) button, a new line of data is displayed. If you keep pushing, you will eventually get the following displays:

$$17 \quad 153 \quad 969$$
$$18 \quad 171 \quad 1140$$

So with the help of a program, our problem is finished. The answers are—

1. There are 969 balls in the pyramid.
2. The pyramid is seventeen levels high.
3. We will need 140 more balls to make the next largest pyramid.

With the calculator, the problem was solved very quickly. If we were to change 1000 balls to 1 000 000 balls, we could get the answer by continually pushing the EXE button and watching the display. This seems to be a mindless waste of time, similar to working out the original table with pencil and paper. With a slight change in our program, we can jump immediately to the answer for 1 000 000:

Add: 35 IF P < 10 ↑ 6 THEN GOTO 50
     45 END
Change: 80 GOTO 35

This passes all the printing of the lesser-sized pyramids. After thirty seconds or so we read

181   16 471   1 004 731.

This means that with 181 levels, there are 16 471 balls in the bottom level and 1 004 731 balls in the pyramid. But this pyramid is 4 731 balls too big. Subtracting the balls in the foundation, 16 471, from the total, 1 004 731, we get the answers to our questions:

1. There are 988 260 balls in the pyramid.
2. The pyramid is 180 levels high.
3. It would take 4 731 more balls to build the next largest pyramid.

OK. I guess the next question is what if we had a billion balls? I suppose this program could solve the problem. It might take 500 minutes on the calculator though. On a computer, we could probably knock it off in a few minutes. Even a trillion balls would be reasonable with a computer. But since there are infinitely many numbers, we will reach a point where even the computers can't cope. And why should they? Large numbers are not the point anyway; we want a formula.

Deductive Phase

The original table displayed a pattern in the T column that may be familiar. The numbers 1, 3, 6, 10, and 15 are appropriately called *triangular* numbers, and they are the result of adding strings of consecutive numbers:

1, 1 + 2, 1 + 2 + 3, 1 + 2 + 3 + 4, 1 + 2 + 3 + 4 + 5, . . .

You may know the formula for $1 + 2 + 3 + \ldots + N$ to be $N(N + 1)/2$. If you plug in 17 for N, you get (17) 18/2 = 153, the number of balls in the foundation level of our original problem.

The numbers in the P column of our table are called, coincidentally, *pyramidal* numbers. To find a formula for these is not easy unless you know what to look for. Here are two techniques that can be applied.

The technique of finite differences has wide application in searching for formulas to fit patterns in a list. In fact, it will work exactly when the formula is a polynomial. It simply takes the differences of the differences of the differences of the differences, and so on, of successive numbers in a list, until the ultimate differences become a constant, if they ever do. The chart in figure 3.4 shows how this technique works in our problem. The row labeled $D(1)$ lists the successive differences of the pairs in the top row. $D(2)$

does the same for the second row, $D(3)$ does this for the third row. We stop at $D(3)$ because we have reached a constant, 1. It should be no surprise that row $D(1)$ is the list for T, the triangular numbers, and row $D(2)$ is the list for N, the level numbers. After all, that was the way the list for P was formed.

P	1		4		10		20		35		56
$D(1)$		3		6		10		15		21	
$D(2)$			3		4		5		6		
$D(3)$				1		1		1			

Fig. 3.4

The technique tells us that the original list is satisfied by a cubic polynomial, that is, $P(N) = aN^3 + bN^2 + cN + d$ for some coefficients a, b, c, and d. In general, if a constant is reached after n successive differences, then the original list can be written $f(1)$, $f(2)$, $f(3)$, . . ., where f is an nth-degree polynomial. Finding the relationship between the entries in the difference lists and the coefficients of the polynomial makes a very nice exploratory problem.

We can put in four values for N and P and find the coefficients a, b, c, and d, but we prefer to introduce another technique. It has a more limited application, but it works nicely here. We shall call this the technique of successive ratios:

P	1		4		10		20		35		56
Ratio		4/1		10/4		20/10		35/20		56/35	
Reduced		4/1		5/2		2/1		7/4		8/5	

If we change the 2/1 to 6/3, we see a nice pattern. The next ratio in the list would be 9/6 (3/2), so the next number in the P list should be (3/2)56. That converts to 84, and we know that to be correct. The next one after 84 should be (10/7)84 = 120. This too is correct. Now let us write the formula:

$P(1) = 1$
$P(2) = (4/1)1 = 4$
$P(3) = (5/2)4 = 10 = (5/2)(4/1)$
$P(4) = (6/3)10 = 20 = (6/3)(5/2)(4/1)$
$P(5) = (7/4)20 = 35 = (7/4)(6/3)(5/2)(4/1) = (7 \times 6 \times 5)/(3 \times 2 \times 1)$
$P(6) = (8/5)35 = 56 = (8 \times 7 \times 6)/(3 \times 2 \times 1)$
.
.
.
$P(N) = (N + 2)(N + 1)(N)/(3 \times 2 \times 1)$

Let us try it. $P(17) = (19 \times 18 \times 17)/(3 \times 2 \times 1) = 969$. That checks. $P(180) = (182 \times 181 \times 180)/(3 \times 2 \times 1) = 988\ 260$. That checks. It must be right, and furthermore, it even looks like a generalization of the formula for triangular numbers:

$$T(N) = (N + 1)(N)/(2 \times 1)$$

Creative Phase

If you read this discussion without trying any ideas of your own, you may not have thought of questions along the way. However, you may have noticed some curious things. Here are some possibilities. You should add your own to this list.

1. What would happen if we wanted to build square pyramids with the tennis balls? Are there other shaped pyramids besides triangular and square?

2. Suppose we wanted to build more pyramids out of the leftover balls. For example, when we started with 1000 balls, 31 were left over after the big 969-ball pyramid. These could make a 20-ball pyramid, a 10-ball pyramid, and a single-ball "pyramid." That makes four pyramids in all. Try this idea of successive pyramid building with other numbers.

What number of balls less than 1000 gives the greatest number of successive pyramids?

3. As we have noticed, the formulas for triangular and pyramidal numbers are similar. Are there other examples of similar algebraic formulas for similar geometric objects (in two and three dimensions)? Can we extend the formula for triangular and pyramidal numbers to higher dimensions and make sense of it (either geometrically or numerically)?

This concludes our mathematical excursion. It was a short trip, made even shorter by the programmable calculator. In fact, it was so short that it was more like a description of a trip than a real-life trip. This trip introduced you to the world of mathematical exploration, but there is no substitute for doing the exploring yourself.

4

A MATHEMATICAL EXPEDITION

In this chapter we will go on a mathematical expedition. This expedition should give a good indication of what a more extensive exploration is like. It is important to note that our particular approach to this problem is just one of many that are possible. One of the great things about these explorations is that they can be as varied as the students who do the exploring.

The title of the problem we have chosen supposes that numbers have personalities. In several problems in the book we treat numbers like people. This is reasonable enough to us because as we work with them, they become friends.

Numbers with Multiple Personalities

All numbers have personalities. In this problem, we examine the rectangular personalities of numbers. The *rectangular personalities* of a number N are the rectangular arrays that can be formed from N dots. For example, the number 4 has one such array as does the number 6, and 12 has two arrays (see fig. 4.1). We shall assume that the 2-by-3 array for 6, shown in figure 4.1, is not different from a 3-by-2 array because one can be formed from the other by a rotation of the figure. Also, we shall say that the number 2 has no rectangular arrays because we will interpret the arrangement • • as a linear array, not a rectangular array. In fact, all prime numbers are like 2 in this regard; they do not have rectangular arrays.

```
• •        • • •      • • • • •        • • • •
• •        • • •      • • • • •        • • • •
                                       • • • •
```

Fig. 4.1

24

THE QUESTION

Of all numbers less than 1 million, which has the most rectangular personalities?

A BEGINNING

As with most explorations of natural numbers, you begin at the beginning; that is, you gather your data from the first several natural numbers 1, 2, 3, 4, and so on.

Figure 4.2 shows a chart listing the composite numbers up to 50 along with the number of different rectangular personalities. The winners for the largest number of personalities are the numbers 36 and 48, with four apiece.

Number N	Rectangular personalities	Number N	Rectangular personalities
4	1	28	2
6	1	30	3
8	1	32	2
9	1	33	1
10	1	34	1
12	2	35	1
14	1	36	4
15	1	38	1
16	2	39	1
18	2	40	3
20	2	42	3
21	1	44	2
22	1	45	2
24	3	46	1
25	1	48	4
26	1	49	1
27	1	50	2

THE EXPLORATION

Inductive Phase

Making a chart like this can teach you a lot of things. For example, you may notice that the dimensions of the rectangles associated with a number are just the nontrivial factors of that number. As you see for the number 48, the dimensions come in pairs 2 × 24, 3 × 16, 4 × 12, and 6 × 8. The

product of each pair of numbers is 48. The trivial factors 1 and 48 do not
form a rectangular array. So the number of rectangular personalities of 48
is half the number of nontrivial factors. Things are not quite as simple as
this for 36, however. Notice that for the number 36, although the dimensions
also come in pairs, 2×18, 3×12, 4×9, and 6×6, one of the factors,
6, is used twice. Thus for 36, the number of nontrivial factors is odd, and
to get the number of rectangular personalities, you must add 1 to the
nontrivial factors before taking one-half of the total. This is true for all
numbers that are perfect squares.

There is a well-known formula for the number of factors (both trivial and
nontrivial) of a natural number. For the purposes of this search we will
assume that we know this formula, although the exploration to find it is an
excellent problem in its own right. Furthermore, once you know the formula,
trying to understand why it works is also an excellent exercise.

If the number N is broken down into the product of its prime powers like
this: $N = p_1^{n_1} p_2^{n_2} \ldots p_k^{n}$, then the total number of factors is $(n_1 + 1)$
$(n_2 + 1) \ldots (n_k + 1)$.

For example, $48 = 2^4 3^1$; so the number of factors is $(4 + 1)(1 + 1) =$
10. Now two of these factors, 1 and 48, are trivial; so eight are nontrivial.
One-half of 8 is 4, the answer we already found. For 36, we have $36 = 2^2 3^2$;
so the number of factors is $(2 + 1)(2 + 1) = 9$. Subtracting the two trivial
factors, we get 7; adding 1 for the square number, we get 8; and taking half
of that, we arrive at 4.

The question about multiple rectangular personalities comes down to a
question of the quantity of factors of a number. We would like to maximize
this quantity in the domain of numbers less than 1 000 000.

As you study the chart, you will notice that the numbers 4, 12, 24, and
36 have the most rectangular personalities of all numbers less than or equal
to themselves. In other words, they are the record holders of their time. So
it might be useful to study the properties of these record holders. One
property is that they are made up entirely of 2s and 3s; that is, the primes
in the decomposition are simply the primes 2 and 3; $4 = 2^2$, $12 = 2^2 3$,
$24 = 2^3 3$, and $36 = 2^2 3^2$. So we shall take our cue from this and look at
large numbers that are less than 1 000 000 and made up of only 2s and 3s.
This approach can be done nicely with a hand calculator.

We begin by finding the largest power of 2 that is less than 1 000 000; it
is 2^{19}, which equals 524 288. This number has twenty factors. If we replace
three of those 2s by two 3s, we get $2^{16} 3^2$; and this is about the same size as
before (actually 9/8 bigger). This number has fifty-one factors, a definite
improvement. Doing this trick again, we get $2^{13} 3^4$, which is slightly bigger
again and has seventy factors. Repeating this we get $2^{10} 3^6$, which has seventy-
seven factors, and $2^7 3^8$, which has seventy-two factors. We have reached the
end of the line with this approach; this last number is no good to us because

it has fewer factors than the previous one.

But if we introduce a new prime, 5, into the scheme, we may get new and better results. Let us take $2^{10}3^6$ and replace 2^2 by 5. Now the new number, $2^8 3^6 5^1$, is bigger by a factor of 5/4 (we should always check to see if the number is less than 1 000 000—this one is 933 120) and has 126 factors. Because we are close to 1 000 000, we shall alter our latest number by replacing 2×3 by 5. The result is the number $2^7 3^5 5^2$, and it has 144 factors. Not bad!

Continuing this kind of experimentation using the next primes, 7, 11, and 13, we find the results in figure 4.3. Let $N_1 = 2^7 3^5 5^2$.

Alteration	Result	New number	Number of factors
replace 2×3 by 7	$(7/6)N_1$	$N_2 = 2^6 3^4 5^2 7^1$	210
replace $2^2 3$ by 11	$(11/12)N_2$	$N_3 = 2^4 3^3 5^2 7^1 11^1$	240
replace 3×5 by 13	$(13/15)N_3$	$N_4 = 2^4 3^2 5^1 7^1 11^1 13^1$	240
replace 2^2 by 5	$(5/4)N_4$	$N_5 = 2^2 3^2 5^2 7^1 11^1 13^1$	216
replace 3×5 by 17	$(17/15)N_5$	$N_6 = 2^2 3^1 5^1 7^1 11^1 13^1 17^1$	192

Fig. 4.3

Reviewing the table, we see that N_3 and N_4 are the best choices. N_5 and N_6 have fewer factors, and furthermore, N_6 is 1 021 020, which is too big. We shall go back to our two leaders, N_3 and N_4, and change them a bit, as in figure 4.4.

Alteration	Result	New number	Number of factors
for N_3, replace 5 by 2×3	$(6/5)N_3$	$N_7 = 2^5 3^4 5^1 7^1 11^1$	240
for N_4, replace 3 by 2^2	$(4/3)N_4$	$N_8 = 2^6 3^1 5^1 7^1 11^1 13^1$	224
replace 13 by 3×5	$(15/13)N_7$	$N_9 = 2^6 3^2 5^2 7^1 11^1$	252

Fig. 4.4

Unfortunately, the last number, N^9, is larger than 1 000 000; it is 1 108 800. On the basis, then, of what we have in the table, the winners are $N_3 = 831 600$, $N_4 = 720 720$, and $N_7 = 997 920$. All have 240 factors, 238 nontrivial factors, and 119 rectangular personalities. I suppose that if you want to break the tie, we should choose the smallest of the three numbers, 720 720, as the winner; after all, it is the first number to achieve the 240 mark.

Our original problem is now solved. The greatest number of rectangular personalities is 119, and three numbers share it. We have not proved this fact, but we have demonstrated it in a convincing fashion. After all, what other number could possibly beat our three winners?

The exploration above is just one of many possible explorations. All explorations must end with the right answers, but there are many different roads to the correct solution, and the methods of establishing the solution can be very different. This probably explains why the mathematical language has so many adjectives to describe a solution to a problem: *elegant, elementary, elaborate, straightforward, computational, beautiful, simple, complex, tedious, technical,* and *ingenious,* to name a few.

Deductive Phase

It is natural to wonder how we would proceed if the number in our original question were larger than 1 million—like 1 billion or 1 trillion or, for that matter, N, where N stands for any number. We could continue to use the method of swapping prime powers as we did before, but with larger numbers, this method could get unwieldy if we could not find a shortcut.

One direction we could take would be to examine the so-called record holders—those numbers that have more factors than any of their predecessors. In fact, we did this for the record holders up to 36 and found them to be composed of only 2s and 3s. We now know that the record holder among the first million numbers is 720 720, which contains 2s, 3s, a 5, a 7, an 11, and a 13. What can we say about the prime decomposition of the record holders? Let us make a list of them (see fig. 4.5). In our listing we shall record the number of factors, not the number of rectangular personalities.

Record holder	Prime decomposition	Number of factors
2	2	2
4	2^2	3
6	2×3	4
12	$2^2 3$	6
24	$2^3 3$	8
36	$2^2 3^2$	9
48	$2^4 3$	10
60	$2^2 3 \times 5$	12
120	$2^3 3^1 5$	16
180	$2^2 3^2 5$	18
240	$2^4 3^1 5$	20
360	$2^3 3^2 5$	24
720	$2^4 3^2 5$	30
840	$2^3 3^1 5 \times 7$	32

Fig. 4.5

The record holders are the same numbers, with the one exception of 48—a record holder among the factor counters, but not among the rectangular personality counters.

The list in figure 4.5 contains all the record holders less than 1000. There are several questions we can ask as we extend this list.

Notice that 3 makes its first appearance as a prime factor in the number 6, whereas 5 appears first in 60 and 7 first in 840. Is there something about the factorization that tells us when we need a new prime factor?

Question. When does 11 first appear? How about 13? How about 17? Can you predict the first appearance of a new prime?

Notice as you read down column 2 in figure 4.5, that the exponents of 2 and 3, respectively, progress as follows: 2, 1; 3, 1; 2, 2; 4, 1. This repeats with the prime 5 added to the factorization but includes further 3, 2 and 4, 2 before 7 is added to the factors.

Question. What can you say about the relationships between the exponents of the primes in the prime factorization of the record holders?

Notice that the numbers in the factor column are themselves numbers with several factors. In fact, the numbers in column 1 all appear somewhere in column 3.

Question. What can you say about the prime decomposition of the numbers in the number-of-factors column?

In order to get an approximation for the number of factors of the record-holding number less than N (for arbitrary N), it would be useful to chart the courses of column 1 and column 3 and compare them.

Question. What can you say about the rate of growth of the numbers in column 1 as compared to column 3?

Analyzing the patterns of the exponents of the record holder is only one approach to solving the general question. There is no guarantee of success if you follow this approach, only the assurance of an exciting mathematical search. And there is another positive aspect—if this approach does not work, it will leave the original question unsolved, which, in turn, will promise several more hours of exciting exploration. And this is good!

Creative Phase

While exploring one problem, other problems suggest themselves. We will follow one lead in detail and suggest others later. The problem "The Genealogy of the Natural Numbers" in chapter 8 examines aspects of this question also.

If you actually drew the rectangular arrays of dots as you examined the rectangular personalities of numbers, it may have occurred to you that each arrangement has contained within it several smaller rectangular arrays. For example, in the 3 × 4 array shown in figure 4.6, we can count eighteen different rectangles (rectangles placed in different locations) and five different shapes of rectangles in the array. There are six 1 × 1  squares,

seven 1 × 2  or 2 × 1  rectangles, two 3 × 1

rectangles, two 2 × 2 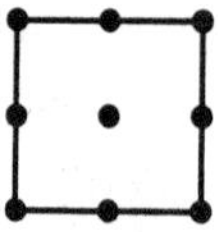 squares, and one 2 × 3

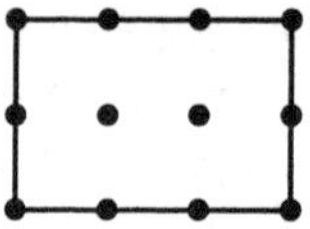

rectangle.

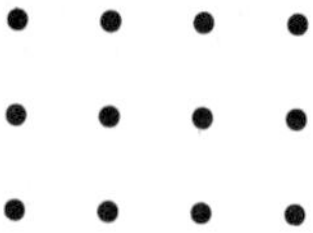

Fig. 4.6

The ultimate question here is, Given a rectangular array of dots with dimensions $N × M$, how many rectangles and how many differently shaped rectangles are contained in the array? In our search for an answer, we will make N and M specific numbers that are large enough to require a thoughtful investigation but not so large that we cannot find an answer.

Question. Given a 50 × 100 array of dots:

  a) How many different rectangles are contained in this array?

  b) How many differently shaped rectangles are contained in the array?

There are various avenues of approach, and we will choose one that organizes data as in figure 4.7 and displays patterns (we hope).

These numbers can easily be worked out by drawing the appropriate rectangle and counting. The number 18 we found in figure 4.6 is underlined twice in figure 4.7, indicating that we already know that there are eighteen different rectangles in a 3 × 4 (or 4 ×3) array of dots.

For a 50 × 100 rectangular array, we see, from the patterns in the chart in figure 4.7, that we need only extend the sequence 0, 1, 3, 6, 10, . . ., 100 places, find that number, and multiply it by the number that occurs in the

The Number of Different Rectangles in an Array

Dots in a row

		1	2	3	4	5	6	7	8	9	10
	1	0	0	0	0	0	0	0	0	0	0
Dots	2	0	1	3	6	10	15	21	28	36	45
in a	3	0	3	9	18	30	45	63	84	108	135
column	4	0	6	18	36	60	90	126	168	216	270
	5	0	10	30	60	100	150	210	280	360	450

Fig. 4.7

fiftieth place of the same sequence. These two numbers are 4950 and 1225, respectively. Their product is 6 063 750.

The formula for the general rectangle of dimension $N \times M$ is the product of the Nth term and the Mth term of the sequence 0, 1, 3, 6, 10, ... The formula for the Nth term of this series is $N(N-1)/2$. Notice that the sequence 0, 1, 3, 6, 10,... is simply the sequence of triangular numbers that we met in chapter 3. So our final answer is that there are $N(N-1)M(M-1)/4$ rectangles contained within an $N \times M$ rectangular array of dots.

We found this result with the help of a chart. For some people, this may not constitute a *proof*. These people should not rest until they have found a convincing argument that explains the answer. One argument can be based on the fact that a rectangle is uniquely determined by the placement of the two dots that lie at the ends of its diagonal.

The chart in figure 4.8, as the one before, is easily made by counting the different shape of rectangles in the given arrays. We have underlined the 5 that we know to be the number of differently shaped rectangles in a 3 × 4 (or 4 × 3) array.

The Number of Differently Shaped Rectangles in an Array

Dots in a row

		1	2	3	4	5	6	7	8	9	10
	1	0	0	0	0	0	0	0	0	0	0
Dots	2	0	1	2	3	4	5	6	7	8	9
in a	3	0	2	3	5	7	9	11	13	15	17
column	4	0	3	5	6	9	12	15	18	21	24
	5	0	4	7	9	10	14	18	22	26	30

Fig. 4.8

Analyzing the chart, we can extend the pattern to the 50×100 rectangle as follows: the 2×100 entry would be 99, the 3×100 entry $99 + 98$, the 4×100 entry $99 + 98 + 97$, and the 50×100 entry would be $99 + 98 + 97 + ... + 51$, which equals 3675.

Extending this analysis to the general case of an $N \times M$ rectangular array of dots (for $N \leq M$) should give us $(M - 1) + (M - 2) + (M - 3) + ... + (M - N + 1)$ differently shaped rectangles. Using the formula for summing an arithmetic series, we get the result $(2M - N)(N - 1)/2$.

As we mentioned in the previous problem, following patterns does not constitute a proof for everyone. If you are one of those for whom it does not, you should keep at it until you find an argument that works for you.

Our original expedition is by no means over at this point. Nevertheless, this chapter is finite; so we will finish with a couple more suggestions. Along with "The Genealogy of the Natural Numbers," two other problems in the book bear directly on this subject. They are "Squares within Squares and Cubes within Cubes" and "Triangles within Triangles" in chapter 7.

Another shape that offers a rich exploration is the trapezoid. For the trapezoid, it is interesting to go back to our initial question with rectangles—the question of multiple personalities. A trapezoidal personality of a number N is an array of N dots arranged in the shape of a trapezoid. For example, 9 dots can be arranged in two different ways:

Question. Of all the numbers less than 1 000 000, which has the most trapezoidal personalities?

Finally, and most important, you should investigate problems of your own creation. Solving someone else's problems is fun, but finding your own problems and then solving them makes you a true explorer in the field of mathematics.

As we look back over our expedition, we notice some surprising features. The original question that we posed was answered, but the answer was reached inductively and was not conclusively established deductively. Furthermore, the generalization of the question, that is, "Of all numbers less than N, which has the most rectangular personalities?," was not answered at all. Also, the creative part of the exploration was as extensive as the inductive and deductive parts. We started with one question, did not answer it conclusively, and finished with many more questions.

There is a lesson here: producing answers is important, but the search for the answer is more important. Too often, students are asked to get answers and to get them quickly. This injects an urgency and a competitiveness into doing mathematics. Furthermore, most mathematical problems are made to fit this scenario. Such problems are closed ended, admit one approach, and have a single answer.

Doing mathematics is not a competition and not a race. It is a complicated thought process. The problems in this book are meant to call on the full range of mathematical thinking. For this thinking to prosper, time constraints must be removed. The student should feel free to savor the exploration, experiment with various approaches and compare them, and pursue related questions and try to solve them. If all the loose ends are not tied down and all the related questions are not answered—well, that is as it should be. There is no expiration date on the problems in this book. They will always be there to be revisited in the future.

5

A COMPUTER-ASSISTED EXPLORATION

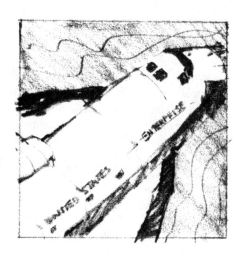

The excursions in chapter 6 and the expeditions found in chapter 7 can be carried out, in most cases, with just a pencil and paper—lots of paper. In some situations this is the only alternative. Often, however, the computer can be very helpful. It can generate data that can lead to pattern recognition, and it can handle lengthy and tedious arithmetic calculations.

There are some explorations where the computer is the natural tool to use. These are the problems found in chapter 8. The computer-assisted explorations are problems that rely on the computer or programmable calculator for at least half the solution. Here we will explore, in detail, an example of a problem that depends almost entirely on the calculator and the computer.

This example nicely demonstrates the two different ways that the computer can be used in the problems of chapter 8. The computer can be used as a super calculator, and it can be used as a simulator. As a super calculator, the computer can handle those types of calculations that will take forever when attempted by hand. (In fairness to calculators, it should be pointed out that inexpensive hand calculators can often do the job and programmable calculators can usually do the job required in these problems.) As a simulator, the computer samples a portion of an incredibly large number of possible outcomes and produces an average or an expected value.

Exploration with a computer can be creative and enlightening. But the computer can also deal a preemptive strike to creativity and curiosity. There is a right way and a wrong way to explore with the computer. As strange as it sounds, the right way parallels the way we explore with pencil and paper. With pencil and paper, we try things out, we follow different paths and patterns, and we do this over a period of time—often very slow time. The computer compresses the time frame drastically. If we let it, it will wipe out the exploration experience entirely. It will hand us our answer without so much as a pat on the back or, worse yet, without so much as a glimpse into the nature of the problem. So when we use the computer, we must sometimes slow it down, follow its processes, watch the patterns develop on the screen, and maybe even stop to smell the subtleties. And finally, even while the computer is busily working away, we must be sure to keep pencil and paper handy. There still is no better way to gain mathematical insight than to try out our ideas on paper.

Birthdays Are Not That Uncommon

I was eating at a restaurant the other night when suddenly people started singing "Happy Birthday" to a child at another table. What a coincidence, I thought. There couldn't be more than fifty people in the restaurant and one of them has a birthday on this very day! Maybe someone in here has the same birthday as I have, 17 January. Naw! That would be a long shot. But I will bet that there are a pair of people in here right now with the same birthday. Maybe there are several pairs. There might even be three people in here with the same birthday. In any case, I'll bet there are more than two people that share a birthday. On second thought, maybe this whole thing is not a coincidence after all. Maybe this child was at this restaurant especially because of the birthday. Maybe all my thinking was just silly dreaming. It wouldn't be the first time.

THE QUESTIONS

In a group of fifty people—

1. What are the chances that one of them has my birthday?

2. What are the chances that two people have the same birthday?

3. What are the chances that there are three people with the same birthday?

4. On average, how many of these people will share a birthday with someone else?

A BEGINNING

Suppose we ask the questions for a group of three people about the seasons of their birthdays. There are four seasons, winter, spring, summer, and fall. For short, we will label them A, B, C, D. We will label the people 1, 2, and 3. Different possible birth-season scenarios can be denoted by sequences of triples like this: ABB, CAA, BBC, ACB, and so on. There are, in all, sixty-four birth-season possibilities because each of the three people could have any of four birth seasons, and $4 \times 4 \times 4 = 64$. There are twenty-seven possible scenarios that do not include season A, my birth season. This is because persons 1, 2, and 3 can have three available seasons different from A. So the chances that at least one person has birth season A is $1 - 27/64 = 37/64$.

Out of the sixty-four total possibilities, the following eighteen show all different birth seasons:

ABC	BCA	CAB	CBA	BAC	ACB
ABD	BDA	DAB	DBA	BAD	ADB
BCD	CDB	DBC	DCB	CBD	BDC

Of the other forty-six, there are four possible ways that three can share a season: AAA, BBB, CCC, DDD. Forty-two of the outcomes are single matched pairs. So the chances that at least two people share the same birth season are $46/64 = 23/32$; the chances that exactly two share the same season are 42/64, or 21/32; and the chances that three were born in the same season are $4/64 = 1/16$. On average there are

$$(1/64) ((0 \times 18) + (2 \times 42) + (3 \times 4)) = 96/64 = 1.5$$

people in a group of three that share a birth season with someone else.

THE EXPLORATION

Inductive Phase

The birthday problem is a familiar one, and questions 1 and 2 have easily derived formulas that provide exact answers.

The chances that fifty people all have a birthday different from mine are simply $1 - (364/365)^{50}$. An inexpensive hand calculator tells us that this is about 12.8 percent.

For question 2, the chances that all fifty people have birthdays different from each other are

$$(365/365) (364/365) (363/365)...(316/365).$$

This product is awkward but manageable on the same calculator—it is about 2.9 percent. So the chances that at least two people share a birthday are $100 - 2.9 = 97.1$ percent.

Since questions 3 and 4 are not handled by familiar formulas, we will turn to the computer for help. To familiarize ourselves with our high-powered assistant, we will use it on all four parts of the problem, checking its effectiveness on the first two parts, which have exact answers that we know.

We will employ the technique of computer simulation. In this process the computer gathers data for us. Instead of listing various possibilities as we did in the explanation above, the computer will create a few scenarios and sample them for us. There are 365^{50} (a number with well over 100 digits) possible scenarios of birthdays among fifty people. In our programs we will ask the computer to generate some of the possibilities and average the findings.

We will create our programs in BASIC. These programs will simulate the situations in questions 1, 2, 3, and 4. The programs will gather NT (numbers of trials) different groups of N random numbers between 1 and 365, and then check for number matches. The following program goes through 1000 trials of groups of fifty random numbers and checks to see if there are any number matches. This simulates the process of checking to see if anyone in a group of fifty people has my birthday (in the program we make my birthday the number 1).

```
      PROGRAM 1
100 NT = 1000
110 N = 50
120 S = 0
130 FOR I = 1 TO NT
140 FOR J = 1 TO N
150 K = INT(RND(1))*365 + 1)
160 IF K = 1 THEN S = S + 1 : J = N
170 NEXT J
180 NEXT I
190 PRINT S/NT
```

Line 150 generates the random numbers between 1 and 365. Line 160 says that if a number matches the number 1, then count it $(S = S + 1)$ and move on to the next group of fifty numbers. A running total of matches is kept, and line 190 reads out on the screen the average number of matches in 1000 trials.

Running this program, we get $S/NT = .139$. In this experiment, the number 1 was matched 139 times out of 1000. In terms of birthdays, this means that the experimental average is 13.9 percent that 17 January will be someone's birthday in any random group of fifty people. This is disturbing news. We already know the answer to be 12.8 percent, and 13.9 percent is not that close. Perhaps this simulation method isn't all that great.

Moving to question 2 with computer simulation, we use the following program:

```
      PROGRAM 2
100 DIM B(365)
110 INPUT "NT=", NT
120 N = 50
130 S = 0
140 FOR I = 1 TO NT
150 FOR J = 1 TO 365 : B(J) = 0 : NEXT J
```

```
160 FOR J = 1 TO N
170 K = INT(RND)(1)*365 + 1)
180 B(K) = B(K) + 1 : IF B(K) > 1 THEN S = S + 1 : J = N
190 NEXT J
200 NEXT I
210 PRINT S/NT
```

This program assigns the numeral 0 to all numbers 1 through 365 (line 150). As the fifty random numbers are generated, a 1 is assigned to each number as it occurs. When a number occurs twice, a 2 is assigned, a match is recorded, and we move on to the next group of fifty (line 180).

Running this program with input $NT = 1000$, we get $S/NT = .963$. This agrees more closely with our theoretical answer (.971); so we can feel somewhat better, but not altogether enthusiastic, about the simulation approach.

Turning to question 3, we realize that we must place our trust in the computer. We have no theoretical backup; we are forced to accept the simulation answer. The program we use is similar to program 2, the only difference being in line 180 where the 1 is changed to a 2 to signify that we will be counting matched triples rather than matched pairs. The new line 180 reads

```
180 B(K) = B(K) + 1 : IF B(K) > 2 THEN S = S + 1: J = N.
```

Running this program for $NT = 1000$, we find that $S/NT = .121$. If this is at all accurate, we can expect that about 1/8 of the time there will be a triple birthday match in a group of fifty people.

For question 4, we can use the following program. Again it is like program 2 with an alteration in line 180. The new line 180 deletes the "$J = N$" command because we are interested in finding all the matches that occur in fifty numbers rather than simply the first match. Also we shall insert a new line, 185, to take into account the contingency of multiple matches, in particular, a triple match ($B(K) > 2$) and a quadruple match ($B(K > 3)$) (if, by some miracle, there were one). Minor changes in lines 130 and 210 are also needed:

```
130 S = 0: T = 0: U = 0
180 B(K) = B(K) + 1 : IF B(K) > 1 THEN S = S + 1
185 IF B (K) > 2 THEN T = T+1 : IF B(K) > 3 THEN U = U + 1
210 PRINT S/NT, T/NT, U/NT
```

Running this program for $NT = 500$, we get $S/NT = 3.126$, $T/NT = .118$, $U/NT = 0$. To extract the distinct pairs that are not triples, we subtract $3.126 - 0.118$ and get 3.008. So in a group of fifty people, we can expect slightly more than three birthday-matched pairs. This result also confirms that our answer to question 3 is good. Here we get .118 for the probability of a triple birthday match. For the average we have

$$2(3.008) + 3(.118) = 6.37$$

people with a shared birthday.

These are examples of programs that give just the answers. Since the first part of the exploration concentrates on finding answers, we may stop here, at least temporarily, until we hire an investigation team to check out the reliability of our high-tech assistant.

Deductive Phase

This part of the exploration focuses on the meaning of, and the reasons for, our answers.

Our first order of business is an analysis of the accuracy of our computer-simulation technique.

Let us look at question 1 again. The answer is 12.8 percent. Maybe 1000 trials were not enough. Let us try 2000 and keep track of the variation of the answers as we go along. This can be accomplished by altering program 1 slightly. We change line 100 and insert a new line, 175, to keep track of our progress after every 100 trials:

```
100 NT = 2000
175 IF INT(I/100) = I/100 THEN PRINT I,S/I
```

You may delete line 190. The readout is in figure 5.1.

100	.14	1100	.138
200	.15	1200	.1433
300	.1433	1300	.1433
400	.1525	1400	.141
500	.146	1500	.142
600	.15	1600	.1425
700	.1443	1700	.14
800	.14	1800	.142
900	.14	1900	.142
1000	.139	2000	.1405

Fig. 5.1

Our findings are disturbing. The variation in the answers above is not great, and the answer is, and apparently will stay, about 14 percent.

Maybe the problem lies with the random-number process; perhaps it has a preference for the number 1. Let us try other numbers. Here are the results of choosing a number other than 1 for our fixed number. We changed the 1 in line 160 of program 1 to 99, then 347, and then 183. The results are as follows:

For $K = 99$, $S/NT = .136$
$K = 347$, $S/NT = .114$
$K = 183$, $S/NT = .129$

This test leads us to believe that our random-number generator is biased. Maybe we can get around this. Let us arrange for new groups of fifty numbers to match different given numbers. We can do this by altering line 160 of program 1 as follows:

160 IF K = INT(I*(365/1001) + 1) THEN S = S+1 : J = N

Under this scheme, as the program runs from 1 to 1000, the number to be matched runs, as uniformly as possible, from 1 to 365.

Running this program, we get $S/NT = .128$. It worked! This answer is the same as the theoretical answer.

Turning to question 2, we will find out if 2000 trials get us closer to the theoretical answer than 1000 did. As with question 1, we will keep track of the variation in our answers after every 100 trials. The program is like program 2 with the following change:

195 IF INT(I/100) = I/100 THEN PRINT I, S/I

You may dispense with line 210.
Running this program with $NT = 2000$ yields the result in figure 5.2.

100	.96	1100	.9645
200	.955	1200	.965
300	.9567	1300	.9669
400	.9575	1400	.9693
500	.962	1500	.9693
600	.9567	1600	.9713
700	.9586	1700	.9712
800	.9625	1800	.9711
900	.9611	1900	.9711
1000	.963	2000	.97

Fig. 5.2

This result is a success. The computer answer of 97 percent is close to the theoretical answer of 97.1 percent. Furthermore, the successive checks on the progress of the answer show that the variation gets smaller and the simulation answer hones right in on the correct answer. This is reassuring.

Although we feel good about our answer to question 3, let us use this same device and print out twenty approximations of the answer, as we did above. Doing this requires altering line 180 slightly. Change IF B(K) > 1 to IF B(K) > 2.

The results of this experiment are in figure 5.3.

100	.12	1100	.12
200	.13	1200	.1175
300	.1333	1300	.12
400	.135	1400	.12143
500	.126	1500	.12267
600	.1367	1600	.12188
700	.1342	1700	.11882
800	.1286	1800	.11778
900	.1256	1900	.11684
1000	.121	2000	.116

Fig. 5.3

The answer for question 3 becomes 11.6 percent. That is our expectation that there will be three matching birthdays in a group of fifty people. The variation is a little more than we like, but it looks as if this answer is probably correct to within .4 percent. It might be a good idea to try 5000 trials, but we will not do that here.

So far we have spent our time looking at the behavior of the computer. Is it trustworthy? Accurate? Reliable? Although this background check into our partner's integrity is important, we must not lose sight of our goal—exploring the mathematics.

First we shall take our own advice and slow the computer down a bit. We do this by asking the computer to read out for us what it is doing. Let us watch a cycle of fifty random numbers being generated. The following program does this:

```
100 N = 50
110 FOR J = 1 to N
120 K = INT(RND(1)*365 + 1)
130 LPRINT J,K
140 NEXT J
```

We use the command "LPRINT" instead of "PRINT" only because we want to print the fifty numbers on paper. They go by on the screen too fast for us to read them.

The list we get is in figure 5.4.

This is the raw material. I defy you to quickly pick out all the matches of random numbers. There are matched pairs here, however—four of them. The fifth and forty-eighth numbers match, as do the numbers corresponding to 8 and 23, 11 and 20, and 29 and 39. This raises some questions: Are four matches typical? The first match occurs at the twentieth person, the second occurs at the twenty-third person. Is that typical? The answer to question 4 partially answers the first question; there are, on average, just over three matches per fifty numbers. The second question is not yet answered.

1	45	11	257	21	271	31	188	41	209
2	238	12	195	22	244	32	206	42	362
3	318	13	355	23	166	33	271	43	106
4	267	14	118	24	122	34	242	44	241
5	292	15	349	25	58	35	85	45	343
6	27	16	342	26	269	36	170	46	139
7	179	17	196	27	199	37	47	47	325
8	166	18	207	28	156	38	178	48	292
9	40	19	245	29	21	39	21	49	346
10	347	20	257	30	281	40	13	50	118

Fig. 5.4

Let us now watch what happens when we follow 100 trials of random collections of groups of fifty numbers. We will print out the matches using this program. It is very similar to program 2.

```
100 DIM B(365)
110 NT = 100 : N = 50
120 FOR I = 1 TO NT
130 FOR J = 1 TO 365 : B(J) = 0 : NEXT J
140 FOR J = 1 TO N
150 K = INT(RND(1)*365 + 1)
160 B(K) = B(K) + 1 : IF B(K) > 1 THEN PRINT I, J, K
170 NEXT J
180 NEXT I
```

Here is the printout of the matches:

1	20	257	4	47	211	8	38	170
1	23	166				8	41	336
1	33	271	5	29	336	8	43	109
1	39	21	5	38	352	8	49	281
1	48	292						
1	50	118	6	10	237	9	11	258
			6	37	147	9	24	85
2	5	81	6	39	279	9	30	193
2	27	341	6	42	229	9	37	40
3	46	310	7	20	224	10	9	321
			7	30	111	10	43	101
4	21	22	7	42	213	10	44	37
4	22	142	7	46	71	10	47	121
4	30	364	7	50	111			
4	33	154				11	23	339
4	46	166	8	30	201	11	35	33

11	36	33
11	50	290
12	14	232
12	48	107
13	43	301
13	48	140
14	26	331
14	46	123
14	48	44
14	49	301
15	34	267
15	46	38
16	27	294
16	30	163
16	41	111
17	44	11
17	47	357
17	49	120
18	12	333
18	28	211
18	42	102
19	25	25
19	40	330
20	8	182
20	13	249
21	17	89
22	24	21
22	27	38
22	38	78
22	45	194
23	20	159
23	49	34

24	6	134
24	18	217
24	31	239
25	40	325
25	43	151
26	27	146
26	31	120
26	46	129
27	30	296
27	32	218
27	50	57
28	12	17
28	26	32
28	29	312
28	48	161
29	19	330
29	21	69
29	32	133
29	40	63
29	43	54
30	28	251
30	40	116
30	47	177
30	48	42
31	18	158
31	27	321
31	29	15
31	45	6
32	5	199
32	9	199
32	31	109
32	34	13
32	46	179
33	6	71
33	17	357

33	22	122
33	42	122
35	15	300
35	16	11
35	36	163
35	41	309
35	44	123
35	47	300
36	30	319
36	38	184
36	41	174
37	25	343
37	27	224
37	29	343
37	31	292
37	37	138
37	38	70
37	41	306
37	46	256
38	23	283
38	28	76
39	41	145
39	46	154
39	47	70
40	10	149
40	24	302
41	28	198
41	37	101
41	43	274
41	48	113
42	30	209
42	37	310
42	38	222
43	21	313

43	44	97	54	7	146	65	37	220
			54	20	18			
44	25	157	54	21	281	66	5	57
44	27	181	54	23	244	66	29	100
44	34	180	54	42	331	66	42	354
						66	45	170
45	34	332	55	28	288			
45	38	332	55	35	118	67	8	259
45	39	147	55	36	347			
45	42	314	55	49	181	68	40	91
						68	42	361
46	36	91	56	12	238	68	44	180
46	40	34	56	25	210			
46	44	200	56	36	200	69	21	227
46	49	167	56	39	217	69	23	71
			56	44	282	69	31	188
47	20	271				69	37	73
47	23	253	57	17	133	69	45	303
47	49	46	57	41	262	69	48	30
						69	50	30
48	35	59	58	20	56			
48	41	278				70	19	1
48	44	277	60	28	257	70	35	281
48	50	267	60	31	258	70	38	43
			60	49	322	70	39	110
49	13	178				70	45	71
			61	22	127			
50	18	269	61	28	127	71	4	202
50	27	73	61	43	359	71	23	245
50	30	57	61	47	101	71	45	328
50	48	257	61	48	232			
50	49	32				72	20	68
			62	34	240	72	29	188
51	19	201	62	43	326	72	30	309
						72	44	116
52	13	282	63	22	101	72	50	292
52	16	282	63	40	10			
52	29	282	63	42	263	73	31	82
52	40	351	63	45	45	73	46	116
52	47	91						
			64	15	339	74	35	357
53	36	267	64	28	200	74	40	175
53	40	142	64	31	296	74	41	348
						74	46	13

75	19	307
75	39	260
75	42	127
76	42	130
76	47	285
77	34	123
77	42	259
78	32	204
78	34	39
78	39	8
78	49	39
79	35	191
79	42	160
80	26	11
80	46	98
80	47	145
80	49	68
81	11	123
81	30	206
81	43	322
82	46	335
83	39	311
83	40	84
83	47	130
84	18	330
84	28	72
84	37	264
84	48	44
85	17	265
85	24	249
85	38	301
85	42	93
85	45	108
86	14	18
86	40	293
86	49	221
87	14	18
87	50	240
88	35	83
89	29	228
89	37	165
89	39	120
90	41	76
91	21	329
91	31	169
91	41	76
91	44	85
92	34	62
92	48	240
93	22	189
93	35	23
94	16	92
94	25	92
94	41	263
95	36	180
95	38	193
96	11	276
96	32	86
96	40	91
97	22	299
97	38	220
98	29	317
98	39	1
99	27	364
99	35	54
99	40	94
100	11	23
100	46	201
100	48	140

Now here is a mass (and mess) of data! We can count 313 entries. They represent instances of number matches. There are 11 instances of matched triples. They are located at the trials numbered 7, 11, 32, 33, 35, 37, 45, 61, 69, 78, and 94. An instance of a matched quadruple is located at number 52. In order to find the number of matched pairs, we must subtract the entries that come from the matched triples (2 entries for each triple) and the matched quadruple (3 entries). Doing this, $313 - 11(2) - 1(3)$, we get 288. From our exploration above, we would have expected 301 matched pairs, 12 matched triples, and no quadruples. As for numbers that "share a birthday," we have $2(288) + 3(11) + 4(1) = 613$, an average of 6.13 as compared with the average of 6.37 from above. Notice also that there are two trials where no match occurred, trial numbers 34 and 59. This corresponds closely with the 3 percent that we found in question 2. So, all in all, things are working out pretty well in this example.

Now let us see what else we can discover from all these data. Notice, for example, that the first match occurs 51 percent of the time at, or before, the twenty-second number in the group of fifty. Let us test what the chances for a matched pair by the twenty-second number should be. We use program 2 with a change from "$N = 50$" to "$N = 22$" in line 120. Running this program with $NT = 1000$, we get .48. Not bad. Running the program again with "$N = 23$," we get .514. So it appears that in a group of twenty-three random numbers, the chances are 51.4 percent that there will be a match.

We can check this calculation with a formula. The chances that there is no match among twenty-two numbers are (365/365) (364/365) ... (344/365) = .524. So the chances for a match are $1 - .524 = .476$. This is close to the computer's .48. The chances for no match among twenty-three numbers are (365/365) (364/365) ... (343/365) = .499, so the chances for a match are $1 - .499 = .501$. So twenty-three is the size of the group that will most closely give us a 50 percent expectation of a birthday match.

This leads to another question: What size group will give us a 50 percent expectation of three matched birthdays? We have no formulas for this at our disposal so we must search. Using program 2 as our base, we once again build a program. For convenience, we will write it out completely:

PROGRAM 3

```
100  DIM B(365)
110  INPUT "NT=", NT
120  FOR N = 5 TO 10
125  M = 10*N
130  S = 0
140  FOR I = 1 TO NT
150  FOR J = 1 TO 365 : B(J) = 0 : NEXT J
160  FOR J = 1 TO M
170  K = INT(RND)(1)*365 + 1)
180  B(K) = B(K) + 1 : IF B(K) > 2 THEN S = S+1 : J = M
190  NEXT J
200  NEXT I
210  PRINT M,S/NT
220  NEXT N
```

With $NT = 100$, the results are as follows:

50	.12
60	.17
70	.42

80	.43
90	.56
100	.61

We will refine our search by honing in on the number 86. We make a small change in program 3:

```
120 FOR N = 42 TO 44
125 M = 2*N
```

The results are these:

84	.466
86	.477
88	.514

Our answer seems to be 87. But we can't try it right away because the computer is temporarily down. Using another computer, we find that at $M = 87$, with $NT = 1000$, $S/NT = .486$. This is not exactly what we wanted, but looking again at the earlier results, we see that there was a far larger jump between 86 and 88 than between 84 and 86. This is odd. Maybe we should get a third opinion, or maybe take more trials. Instead, we shall try our own computer at $M = 87$. This trial requires a slight alteration in program 3—erase line 120, change line 125 to $M = 87$, and erase line 220. We get for $NT = 1000$, $S/NT = .505$. Now what? Do we believe our random-number generator or someone else's? While pondering this dilemma, let us return to question 1.

What size crowd should there be for me to have a 50 percent expectation that someone in the crowd has my birthday, 17 January? Here is a program that will search for this:

```
100 INPUT "NT = ", NT
110 FOR N = 5 to 15
120 M = 20*N
130 S = 0
140 FOR I = 1 TO NT
150 FOR J = 1 TO M
160 K = INT(RND(1)*365 + 1)
170 IF K = INT(I*(365/(NT + 1) + 1) THEN S = S + 1 : J = M
180 NEXT J
190 NEXT I
200 PRINT M,S/NT
210 NEXT N
```

The results for $NT = 500$ are as follows:

100	.234
120	.286

140	.318
160	.37
180	.404
200	.414
220	.462
240	.476
260	.522
280	.524
300	.568

It looks as if $N = 250$ is a good choice. Plugging it in with the requisite changes in the program, we get .476. This can't be right; we got .476 for $N = 240$. I guess that using 500 trials is not really accurate; after all, there are 365^{250} possible scenarios. When there were "only" 365^{50} possibilities, 500 trials were not a bad gauge, but 365^{250} is 365^{50} raised to the fifth power! I suppose that we can experiment with 5000 trials, but the search above took over three hours of running time on our computer. Maybe we should get hold of a faster computer and speed this whole thing up.

Actually, for this problem, we need only an inexpensive hand calculator because, once again, we can use a formula. The chances that N people all have different birthdays from mine are $(364/365)^N$, and letting $Y = 1 - (364/365)^N$, we can chart the progress of Y against N like this:

N	50	100	150	200	250	300
Y	.137	.240	.337	.422	.496	.561

Sharpening our answer, we find that if $N = 252$, $Y = .4992$; and if $N = 253$, $Y = .5005$.

Something has been bothering us throughout the whole exploration. What is the meaning, if any, of the numbers 23, 87, and 253? They are the numbers that mark the 50 percent expectation level for matching birthdays. Obviously, 365, the number of days in a year, is related to these numbers. If we chose as our domain the numbers from 1 to 100, the 50 percent expectation numbers would be different. Is there some sort of pattern relating the 50 percent expectation numbers to the size of the domain of random numbers?

Creative Phase

During this exploration a lot of questions have occurred to us. The raw data alone can be mined for hours. For example, we counted 313 entries in the 100 trials. We noted that 2 trials had no entries. It would be fun to tabulate the distribution of instances of matches within the other 98 trials. Here is what we found:

Number of matched pairs	0	1	2	3	4	5	6	7	8
Number of instances		2	10	25	24	22	12	3	1	1

Now we know that the average number of matches is 3.13. But it is of more interest to us to analyze the meaning of these matches. For example, what does this mean in terms of numbers sharing "birthdays"? Below is the distribution for this. We know that the average number of numbers that share a birthday is 6.13. Keep in mind that the instances of number matches do not necessarily indicate how many different numbers have been matched. For example, trial 7 has five number matches, but the number 111 appears twice, indicating a matched triple. So, instead of ten different numbers that share a match, there are only nine for this trial. They are 20 and its partner (we don't know who the partner is except that it is some number less than 20), 42 and its partner, 46 and its partner, and 30 and 50 and their partner.

Number of numbers that share a birthday

0	2	3	4	5	6	7	8	9	10	11	12	13	14	15

Number of instances

2	10	0	25	1	23	4	19	3	8	1	2	1	0	1

So, discounting the natural dips in the curve at the odd number instances, we see a normal-looking distribution: 2 percent of the time there are no shared birthdays, 2 percent of the time there are thirteen or more; 12 percent of the instances have two or fewer shared birthdays, 13 percent have ten or more; 72 percent of the time the number of numbers sharing birthdays falls in the 4 to 8 range.

Of course all this analysis is for groups of size 50. One could wonder how the average number of shared birthdays changes with the size of the group. Q represents that number in the program below. The following program conducts a search to find the answer, testing groups of 20 to 100. It is basically program 3 with these few changes and additions:

```
120 FOR N = 4 TO 20
125 M = 5*N
130    S = 0 : T = 0 : U = 0 : V = 0
.
.
.
180 B(K) = B(K) + 1 : IF B(K) > 1 THEN S = S+1
182 IF B(K) > 2 THEN T = T+1: IF B(K) > 3 THEN U = U+1
185 IF B(K) > 4 THEN V = V+1.
.
.
.
```

203 $Q = 2*(S/NT - T/NT) + 3*(T/NT - U/NT) + 4*(U/NT - V/NT)$
205 PRINT M; S/NT; T/NT; U/NT ; V/NT ; Q
210 NEXT N

For $NT = 1000$, the results are in table 5.1.

Table 5.1

M	S/NT	T/NT	U/NT	V/NT	Q
20	0.506	0.014	0	0	1.026
25	0.776	0.014	0	0	1.566
30	1.13	0.042	0.002	0	2.304
35	1.56	0.04	0	0	3.16
40	2.01	0.048	0	0	4.068
45	2.586	0.078	0.002	0	5.252
50	3.126	0.118	0	0	6.37
55	3.862	0.202	0.006	0	7.932
60	4.56	0.254	0.016	0	9.39
65	5.334	0.308	0.008	0	10.984
70	6.15	0.366	0.022	0	12.688
75	7.27	0.486	0.022	0	15.048
80	8.04	0.542	0.018	0	16.64
85	9.134	0.68	0.038	0.002	18.978
90	10.228	0.828	0.042	0	21.326
95	11.08	0.904	0.056	0.002	23.112
100	12.415	1.024	0.066	0.002	25.912

We need to refine these data to see how accurate our answers are. The trouble is that the running time for this program was about sixteen hours. This is not so bad when you can run it overnight but not so good if we want to know the answer quickly. Also, this search was on a basis of 1000 trials. We have already learned that this may not be enough trials for large groups such as $N = 100$. Anyway, from what we do have, here are our guesses:

Average number of people sharing birthdays
2	4	6	8	10	12	14	16	18	20	22	24	26

Group size
27	40	48	55	62	68	73	78	83	87	92	97	100

One thing that you always look for when you have two rows of figures is a relationship between the rows. And there seems to be one here: doubling the group size seems to result in quadrupling the average number of shared birthdays. If this were to continue, we would expect that, in a group of 200 people, about half of them would share a birthday. This is because doubling 100 would result in quadrupling 26. It also follows that, in a group of 365 people, we would expect about 350 of them to share a birthday. This is because, on average, 22 people share a birthday in a group of 92, and doubling the group size from 92 to 184 and then again to 368 would result in quadrupling the shared birthdays from 22 to 88 and then to 352. I wonder if this is at all accurate?

Question. How big should a group be so that we can expect half the people to share a birthday with someone?

Question. In a group of 365 people, how many will have unique birthdays?

From the data of table 5.1, we can also figure out how many people would expect to share a birthday with two other people. For a group of 100, we can see that $3(.958) + 4(.064) + 5(.002) = 3.14$, so, on average, three people share birthdays with at least two other people.

Turning back to the raw data, we can check when the matches start occurring within the trials. For example, we already checked and found that 51 percent of the time the first match occurs in the first twenty-two numbers generated. By simple counting, we see that 50 percent of the second number matches occur by the thirty-seventh number and 50 percent of the third number matches occur by the forty-fifth number. Since there are only forty-one instances of four or more matched numbers in our data, we cannot continue using these data.

We went on to show, with a formula, that 23 is, in fact, the size of the group that offers a 50 percent chance for a match—the first match. I wonder about the second match, the third match, and so on?

Question. What should the size of a group be so that there is a 50 percent probability that there are—

  a) two pairs of matching birthdays?

  b) three pairs of matching birthdays?

  c) four pairs of matching birthdays?

  d) five pairs of matching birthdays?

Our final list of suggested questions concerns the size of the group sufficient to expect a 50 percent chance of K matching birthdays. For example, we have found that if $K = 2$ (that is, a matched pair of birthdays), a group of size 23 will be sufficient, and if $K = 3$, then a group of size 87 suffices.

Question. What should the size of the group be so that there is a 50 percent probability that there are—

  a) four matching birthdays?

  b) five matching birthdays?

  c) six matching birthdays?

Many of the questions we have asked in this exploration will be examined again in the exploratory problem "Bring Your Social Security Card." If the answers to the questions do not seem to follow a discernible pattern here, then that exploration could be revealing.

Looking back over this exploration, we see that it is quite different from the expedition of chapter 4. The computer led this exploration from beginning to end, whereas pencil-and-paper calculations guided the expedition. This example, though not entirely typical of the problems of chapter 8, nevertheless gives an excellent insight into the technique of computer simulation and how it is used to attack a problem. Certainly pencil-and-paper calculation would not have gotten far.

Some problems inherent in computer simulation are revealed here: the bias of the random-number generator, the difference in random generators from computer to computer, and the question of accuracy, which bears on the number of trials and, in turn, on the running time. And perhaps the biggest problem of all is the sudden availability of the numbers—raw numbers—without any apparent mathematical underpinning. Of course, this is also the strength of the computer—its ability to generate an incredible quantity of data in a short time.

Actually, it all boils down to the same thing; whether we explore with pencil and paper or with the computer, our problem is sifting and organizing data. We must find a pattern, a formula, a significance to the numbers that we produce.

6

TWENTY MATHEMATICAL EXCURSIONS

1. The Diagonal Intruder

All the rectangular-shaped hotels in the city are agitated; the diagonal intruder is on the loose. The intruder enters the hotel at a corner and works his way along a main diagonal entering all the rooms (unit squares or unit cubes) in his path. The good news is that he doesn't take anything; he just follows the straight and narrow path to the opposite corner.

THE QUESTIONS

1. How many rooms are entered by the intruder if the hotel is a rectangle measuring 15 by 42?

2. How many rooms are entered if the hotel is a three-dimensional rectangular box measuring 12 by 20 by 30?

A BEGINNING

For the 4-by-6 rectangle pictured in figure 6.1, the intruder enters eight unit squares. Notice that when the diagonal passes through the corner of a unit square only, it does not enter the square. The same is true for the three-dimensional hotel. If the diagonal passes through a corner or along an edge of a unit cube, it does not enter the cube.

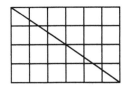

Fig. 6.1

2. Finding the Correct Postage

This question will date the book. When the question was being written, postage was changing from twenty cents to twenty-five cents for first-class letters. Now it is going up to twenty-nine cents. It seems we are always caught with out-of-date stamps. But with clever picking and choosing, we can form the postage each letter needs.

THE QUESTIONS

If we have an unlimited number of twenty-five-cent and twenty-nine-cent stamps, we can form many different denominations of postage.

1. What is the largest denomination we cannot form?
2. What is the largest denomination that can be formed in
   a) only one way?
   b) only two ways?
   c) only three ways?

A BEGINNING

Suppose that our stamps have the denominations of 3 cents and 8 cents. Obviously, we can form postages of 3, 6, 9, 12, 15, 18, 21, ... cents. Also we can form 8, 16, 11, 14, 17, 20, 16, 19, and 22 cents. These denominations can be formed in only one way.

A postage of 35 cents can be formed in two ways: 8, 8, 8, 8, 3 and 3, 3, 3, 3, 3, 3, 3, 3, 3, 8. And a postage of 51 cents can be formed in three ways: 8, 8, 8, 8, 8, 8, 3; 8, 8, 8, 3, 3, 3, 3, 3, 3, 3, 3, 3; and 3, 3, 3, 3, 3, 3, 3, 3, 3, 3, 3, 3, 3, 3, 3, 3, 3.

But 1, 2, 4, 5, 7, 10, and 13 cents cannot be formed at all. So 13 cents is the largest denomination that cannot be formed with 3-cent and 8-cent stamps.

3. Do You Accept Gold Chains?

One year when I was in the minor leagues, I rented a room using a gold chain for the payment. The chain had 365 links, and the rent for the room was 1 link for each day. The understanding was that if I was suddenly called up to the major leagues, I would pay the exact amount due on leaving; otherwise, I would hand over the whole chain at the end of the year. I went to a jeweler and asked him to open up and remove the minimum number of links to give me every possible denomination I might need to pay for my room in the event I was called up early.

THE QUESTIONS

1. What is the minimum number of links that need to be opened and separated so that I can be assured of having the exact rent when I leave?

2. Which links should be removed in the answer to question 1?

Suppose that we have a chain that needs ten links removed to cover all possible contingency payments.

3. What is the maximum length of this chain?

4. Which ten links should be removed so that all possible lengths can be made?

A BEGINNING

Suppose the rental agreement is for one week and the chain has seven links.

In figure 6.2, we see that if the jeweler opens and separates link number 3, then I can form the exact rent for every contingency.

Thus the answer for a seven-link chain is one link. Either link 3 or 5 can be removed.

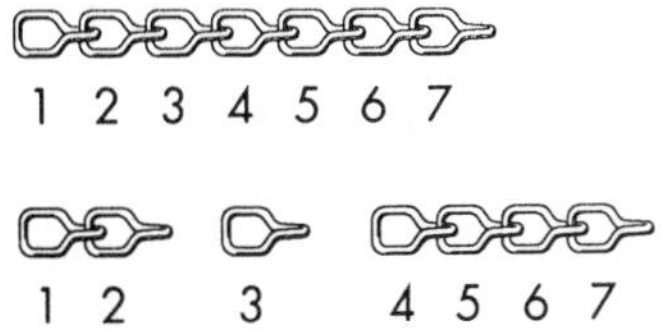

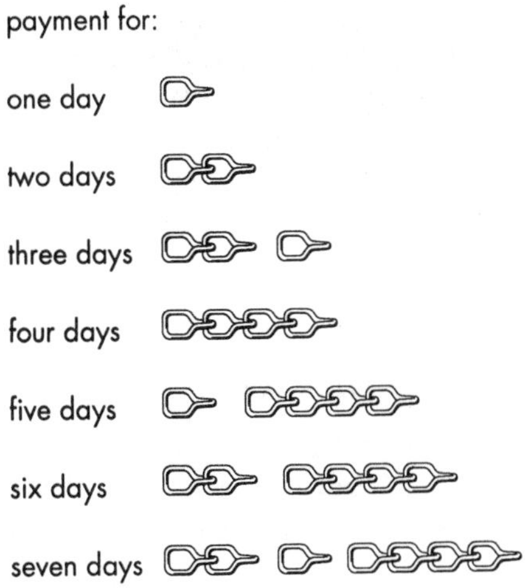

payment for:

one day

two days

three days

four days

five days

six days

seven days

1 2 3 4 5 6 7

1 2   3   4 5 6 7

Fig. 6.2

4. A Circular Massacre

This problem in one form or another has been around for nearly 2000 years—if not longer. Josephus, a Jewish historian of the first century A.D., mentions it. In all its forms, the problem seems to have a violent streak. We are content to keep that in our version.

Imagine thousands of sailors circling the edge of a ship, waiting to be shoved overboard to their deaths in the cold North Atlantic waters. It is not a pretty sight.

THE QUESTIONS

Ten thousand sailors are arranged around the edge of their ship. They hold, in order, the numbers 1, 2, . . ., 10 000. Starting the count with number 1, every other sailor is pushed overboard until they are all gone.

1. Where should you be standing to be the last survivor?

2. How many times is the last survivor skipped over before he is finally pushed overboard?

3. Find the location of the

   a) second to last survivor.

   b) third to last survivor.

   c) 100th to last survivor.

Suppose that the sailors are disposed of in a different way. Where should the last survivor stand if, starting the count with number 1, we push overboard—

4. every third sailor instead of every second sailor as above?

5. every fourth sailor?

A BEGINNING

Suppose that there are ten sailors arranged in a circle. Start the count at number 1 and cross off every other number.

As you can see in the diagrams in figure 6.3, we go around the circle three times. The first time rids us of all even-numbered sailors. The second time knocks off numbers 3 and 7; the third time kills 1 and 9. So number 5 is the last survivor, and he has been skipped over three times. The next to the last to go is number 9.

Fig. 6.3

5. Inverting a Triangle

If you put down three pennies in a triangular shape, you can change the orientation of the triangle by moving a single penny.

The triangle used to be right side up; now it is upside down. That seems easy enough. What is harder to see is that this can be done with any number of pennies. True, you have to move more than one penny, but considering the number of pennies present, it's not bad.

THE QUESTIONS

In a right-side-up equilateral triangle of dots that is 1000 rows deep—

1. What is the minimum of dots that need to be rearranged to form an upside-down equilateral triangle?

2. What percentage of the dots must be rearranged?

A BEGINNING

The triangle in figure 6.4 is four rows deep. Notice that the circled dots in figure 6.4, when rearranged, will form an upside-down triangle that is four rows deep, as in figure 6.5. The dots labeled 1 and 3 have been placed at the ends of the second row of the figure 6.4 triangle, and dot number 2 is moved to the bottom to form a new row.

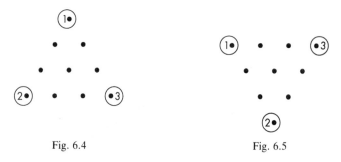

Fig. 6.4   Fig. 6.5

So 3 is the answer to question 1 above for a triangle that is four rows deep. Since there are ten dots present, we have rearranged 30 percent of them.

6. Slicing Cheese

You have in your hand a sharp knife for slicing cheese. You have a large number of guests waiting to be served. Your mission: slice the cheese, making as few cuts as necessary to make pieces for all. Maybe there will be a few pieces left over after everyone leaves.

THE QUESTIONS

There are 10 000 guests at the party. Suppose the cheese is shaped like a flat circular disk.

1. *a)* What is the minimum number of cuts you must make in order to serve all your guests one piece?

b) Some of the cut pieces will contain an undesirable curved edge. How many of these pieces must be served (given you answer to 1*a*)?

Suppose the cheese is a nice sphere.

2. *a)* What is the minimum number of cuts you must make in order to serve all your guests one piece?

b) Some of these pieces contain the undesirable curved boundary. How many of these will have to be served (given your answer to 2*a*)?

A BEGINNING

Suppose we slice a flat circular piece of cheese three times. Figure 6.6 shows that we can create seven regions. Six of these regions contain a circular boundary.

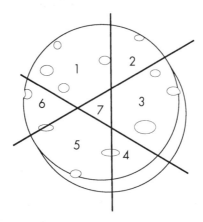

Fig. 6.6

7. Phun with Physics

We have a jar filled with 100 colored balls; 43 are red, 32 are blue, and 25 are yellow. The jar is agitated and the balls are sent hurling about the inside of the jar at a high rate of speed. The speed is so high that, on impact, 2 colliding balls fuse into 1 ball. The color of the newly created ball depends on the color of the 2 colliding balls that formed it in the following way. We shall let R stand for red, B for blue, and Y for yellow.

R, R	→ B	R, B	→ Y
B, B	→ R	R, Y	→ R
Y, Y	→ Y	B, Y	→ B

There are millions of possible sequences of ninety-nine collisions, and the jar can contain many different distributions of colored balls, depending on the collision patterns. After ninety-nine collisions, the jar will contain just one ball.

THE QUESTIONS

1. What is the maximum number of balls that can be in the jar at any one time of the color red? Blue? Yellow?
2. What are the chances that the last ball is red? Blue? Yellow?

A BEGINNING

Suppose that we had 10 balls—5 red, 3 blue, and 2 yellow. One possible sequence of collisions is shown in figure 6.7.

	Collision			Population after collision		
				R	B	Y
1.	R, B	→	Y	4	2	3
2.	Y, Y	→	Y	4	2	2
3.	R, Y	→	R	4	2	1
4.	R, B	→	Y	3	1	2
5.	R, R	→	B	1	2	2
6.	B, Y	→	B	1	2	1
7.	B, B	→	R	2	0	1
8.	R, Y	→	R	2	0	0
9.	R, R	→	B	0	1	0

Fig. 6.7

The maximum number of balls of any color in the jar with this particular sequence is 5 red, 3 blue, and 3 yellow. The last ball in this collision pattern is blue.

8. Number Building
in a World of Unit Fractions

A unit fraction is a fraction that has a numerator of 1. Historically, these fractions have been treated as special numbers. They were used by the Egyptians as the building blocks for all their fractions. Two problems in chapter 7, "Building Numbers the Egyptian Way" and "Cutting a Diamond," treat this theme. Here we explore how unit fractions can be used to build other unit fractions.

THE QUESTIONS

1. Which unit fraction or fractions with denominator $\leq 10\ 000$ can be written in the most ways as the sum of two unit fractions?

2. How many ways can this unit fraction be written?

A BEGINNING

Suppose that the question asked for unit fractions of denominator ≤ 4. With a bit of work we find that—

$1/2 = 1/4 + 1/4$ and $1/3 + 1/6$
$1/3 = 1/6 + 1/6$ and $1/4 + 1/12$
$1/4 = 1/8 + 1/8$, $1/6 + 1/12$, and $1/5 + 1/20$.

So the winner is 1/4. It can be written as the sum of two unit fractions in three ways.

9. Number Necklaces

It's fun to make necklaces, and it doesn't have to be done in art class. It can be done in mathematics class with natural numbers acting as the beads. A number necklace is formed by a sequence of natural numbers that progresses from one to the next by whole-number division or multiplication. The necklace is closed when the sequence returns to its beginning number. For example, figure 6.8 is a necklace of length 7 that contains natural numbers less than or equal to 18.

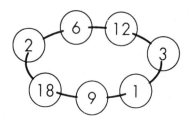

Fig. 6.8

THE QUESTIONS

1. What is the longest necklace that can be formed with the natural numbers ≤ 100? What percentage of the numbers is used?

2. If a necklace is made out of numbers ≤ N, where N ≤ 100, for which N does the longest necklace use—

   a) the largest percentage of the available numbers?

   b) the smallest percentage of the available numbers?

A BEGINNING

Suppose that we form necklaces out of numbers ≤ 20. The necklace in figure 6.8 is such a necklace. For convenience, let us write it this way: 6-12-3-1-9-18-2-6. It has length 7; so 35 percent of the numbers have been used. The necklace 14-7-2-1-14 is of length 4. The necklace 2-8-16-4-20-5-10-1-2 has length 8. It uses up 40 percent of the available numbers—the greatest percentage thus far of the three examples.

10. The Consecutive Index

A whole number stands by itself—simple and complete. Yet mathematicians seem to find it desirable to break a number down into parts. For example, it is always of interest to write a number as a product of its prime factors. In this problem, we examine ways of expressing a number as the sum of consecutive numbers. The number of different ways that a given whole number can be built out of consecutive whole numbers (positive integers) is called its *consecutive index*.

THE QUESTIONS

1. Among the first 10 000 whole numbers, which have the smallest consecutive index? What is that index?

2. Among the first 10 000 numbers, which have the largest consecutive index? What is that index?

3. What can you say about the respective consecutive indices of the numbers N and $2N$?

4. What is the smallest number that has a consecutive index that exceeds 100?

A BEGINNING

Let us look at a simple example—the number 30. After experimentation, we see that $30 = 9 + 10 + 11 = 6 + 7 + 8 + 9 = 4 + 5 + 6 + 7 + 8$. There is no other way to build 30 out of consecutive numbers; so the consecutive index of 30 is 3.

11. Pool, Anyone?

This is the first of three problems in this book about pool. In this problem, the pool table has no pockets. Yet we are asking into which pocket the pool ball falls. In order to answer the questions, we shall assume that the ball is the size of a point and that the pockets are located exactly in the corners and will accept points.

THE QUESTIONS

Suppose we have a pool table that measures 165 by 297. Let us assume that 165 is the vertical dimension and 297 is the horizontal dimension.

1. If we shoot a ball from the lower left corner at a 45° angle—

   a) into which corner does it eventually go?

   b) how many bounces will it take before it goes into the pocket?

   c) how long is the path that it travels?

2. Find a table of different dimensions where the ball goes into the same corner, takes the same number of bounces, and travels the same distance as in 1.

Suppose our table is a square, one unit on a side.

3. Again shooting the ball from the lower left corner, but this time aiming at the point 8/13 up the vertical side at the right—

   a) into which corner will the ball go?

   b) how many bounces will it take before going in?

   c) how long is the path that it travels?

4. At how many points other than 8/13 on the square can you aim that will result in the ball bouncing the same number of times and ending in the same pocket? Are their paths the same length?

A BEGINNING

Suppose we have a 2-by-3 table. Figure 6.9 shows the path of a ball shot at a 45° angle. It bounces three times and then goes into the upper left corner. The path passes diagonally through six squares. Since each diagonal is of length $\sqrt{2}$, the length of the path is $6\sqrt{2}$.

Suppose that the table is square and we shoot the ball from the lower left corner to a point halfway up the vertical side at the right. Then the ball bounces once and ends up in the upper left corner as figure 6.10 shows.

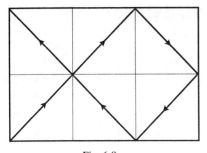 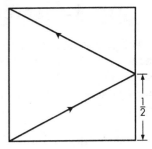

Fig. 6.9   Fig. 6.10

12. Three-dimensional Pool

This is our second pool problem. It is even more ideal than the first. As in the first problem, there are no pockets, the balls are points, and a point disappears only when it hits a vertex exactly. Unlike the first problem, there is no table here. Action takes place inside a rectangular parallelepiped (box). Perhaps it would be better to think of *balls* as *projectiles* bouncing around inside the box. As with pool, we assume that the projectiles bounce perfectly off the interior walls of the box. If one enters a crease (the meeting of two sides), it will bounce off as if striking a plane angled at 45° to the two sides.

THE QUESTIONS

Inside a box measuring 5 by 4 by 3, a projectile is fired along the path of the diagonal of a unit cube from the lower left to the upper right.

1. Into which corner will the projectile go?

2. How many bounces will it take before going into that corner?

3. How long is the path?

In a 1-by-1-by-1 cube, suppose the projectile is aimed at the point (2/3, 3/4) in the *DCGH* plane. We assume that *D* is the origin of that plane. (See fig. 6.11.)

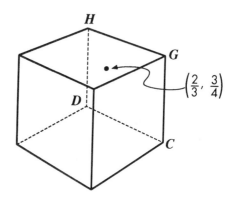

Fig. 6.11

4. Into which corner will the projectile go?

5. How many bounces will it take before it goes into that corner?

6. How long is the path?

A BEGINNING

The box in figure 6.12 is 2 by 2 by 1. The first dimension is in the AB direction; the second, the BC; the third, the CG direction. If you shoot a projectile along the diagonal of a unit cube, it will strike the top of the box as pictured and bounce into the corner at C. Thus, the projectile took one bounce and ended up at C.

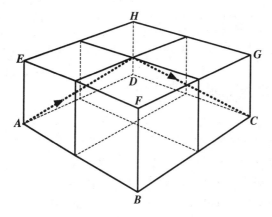

Fig. 6.12

13. What Route Shall I Take Today?

I have accepted a job in the city. I requested that my employer find me a home less than one mile from my workplace so that I could bicycle to work every day. I also wanted my home to be placed so that my trips to work could be along a different route for every day of my contract. My contract is for five years.

THE QUESTIONS

I will work five days a week, fifty weeks a year for five years. The streets in this area form a grid of squares each 1/16 mile on a side; so my home must be fewer than sixteen blocks from work.

1. At how many different sites could my home be located?

2. What is the nearest that I can live to my place of work and still have access to enough different routes?

3. *a*) At what site(s) could I get the maximum number of routes to work?

b) How many years could I work at this job and ride to work along a different route each day if my home is located at a site of maximum routes?

Finding a three-dimensional analogue to this problem is not easy, but fortunately, our friends the prairie dogs can serve the purpose. They live underground in neighborhoods like ours, with streets going in the perpendicular directions of north-south and east-west, but they also build in the up-down direction. Imagine that the job situation is exactly the same as above, that is, a job in the city, a five-year contract, a home less than sixteen blocks away, and a desire to travel to work along a variety of routes.

4. What is the nearest that a prairie dog could live to its place of work and have access to enough different routes?

5. How many years could a prairie dog work at this job if its home is located at a site that allows for a maximum number of routes?

A BEGINNING

Let us start with small numbers and suppose we want a home fewer than five blocks from work that allows for a different route to work every day of the week.

Figure 6.13(a) shows the northeast quadrant of the residential area where I might live. The lines represent streets; the points represent fourteen different intersections that are fewer than five blocks away from *W*, my place of work. We will call these intersections *sites*, near where my home may be located.

Only the site labeled *H* has five or more possible routes. It has six. Figure 6.13(b) shows a sampling of those six routes. The site labeled *P* has only one route to *W*, and *Q* has four different routes. Notice that by "route" we mean a *shortest* path. We do not allow backtracking or going in a direction away from our goal.

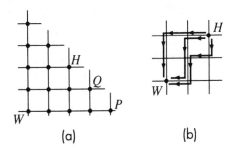

(a)   (b)

Fig. 6.13

So there are four different sites where my home can be located: they are in the *H* position in the directions of NE, NW, SE, and SW from the workplace *W*. The minimum distance I can live from work and get this variety is four blocks; the maximum variety I can achieve by living at this site is six distinct routes.

In the prairie dog community with the same conditions, the answers are quite different. For example, the prairie dog can live three blocks away, as figure 6.14(a) shows, and have six different routes from home to work. In fact, if it lives four blocks away, it can have twelve different routes. Figure 6.14(b) shows an example of this. You can count the different paths.

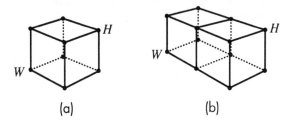

(a)   (b)

Fig. 6.14

14. The Square Root of 2 or Bust

My $5 hand calculator tells me that $\sqrt{2} = 1.4142135$. I know that this is not the exact answer (a finite decimal expansion cannot give the exact answer), but it should be accurate to seven places. What the eighth decimal is, my calculator doesn't tell me. A higher-priced calculator may give more digits but would be accurate to only nine or ten places, maybe eleven.

But there is a way of finding the next digit no matter how many places you already know. There are fractions that approximate $\sqrt{2}$—far better, in fact, than the fractions displayed by the decimal expansion.

Now the fraction 14 142 135/10 000 000 is close to $\sqrt{2}$—within 5/100 000 000 (or half the size of the denominator), in fact—but its denominator is huge. There are fractions that match this approximating power with much smaller denominators.

THE QUESTIONS

1. Find the fraction with the smallest denominator that matches $\sqrt{2}$ to three places.

2. Find the fraction with the smallest denominator that matches $\sqrt{2}$ to seven places.

3. Find the fraction with denominator less than 10^7 that best approximates $\sqrt{2}$. To how many places do you think it is accurate?

4. Find the first twenty-five numbers in the decimal expansion of $\sqrt{2}$.

5. Complete the following statement: If a/b is a decimal fraction that represents $\sqrt{2}$, it is accurate to within $(1/2)b$, but if a/b is a *precise* fraction, it is accurate to within _____.

A BEGINNING

Let us find which fraction with the smallest denominator agrees with $\sqrt{2}$ to one decimal place, that is, 1.4. First, we try fractions with denominator 2. Of those, 3/2 (1.5) is the best, but it does not do the job. Next, we try denominator 3. Of these, 4/3 (1.3) is the best, but it too fails, as do 5/4 (1.25) and 7/4 for denominator 4. We find our answer with denominator 5. It is 7/5, which is 1.4.

Next, let us find the smallest denominator that approximates $\sqrt{2}$ even more closely than 7/5, that is, closer than 1.4142 − 1.4 = 0.0142. After examining fractions with denominator 6, 7, 8, 9, 10, and 11, we find that 17/12 does the trick: 17/12 = 1.41666. . . . Actually, 10/7 is pretty close (1.4286 − 1.4142 = 0.0144) but not better than 7/5.

Of all fractions whose denominators are less than or equal to 7/5 or 17/12, these are the most accurate in approximating $\sqrt{2}$. We call such fractions *precise* fractions.

15. Primes inside Number Spirals

The prime numbers seem to occur randomly within the sequence of natural numbers. If you display the natural numbers along a straight line, in a rectangular array, or in some other organized fashion, the primes will not occur in a recognizable pattern. But if you use a spiral array, there are some startling surprises. A number spiral is a display of natural numbers that begins with a specific integer and progresses, one number at a time, in a spiral fashion.

THE QUESTION

What is the longest diagonal of prime numbers that you can find in a number spiral?

A BEGINNING

The spiral display in figure 6.15 begins with 3 and ends with 112. Theoretically, the spiral continues indefinitely.

We have outlined some of the prime diagonals. The longest here is six primes.

103	102	101	100	99	98	97	96	95	94	93
104	67	66	65	64	63	62	61	60	59	92
105	68	39	38	37	36	35	34	33	58	91
106	69	40	19	18	17	16	15	32	57	90
107	70	41	20	7	6	5	14	31	56	89
108	71	42	21	8	3	4	13	30	55	88
109	72	43	22	9	10	11	12	29	54	87
110	73	44	23	24	25	26	27	28	53	86
111	74	45	46	47	48	49	50	51	52	85
112	75	76	77	78	79	80	81	82	83	84

Fig. 6.15

16. You Can Get Therapy for Just Pennies

A therapy session is held for 1000 pennies. The pennies are encouraged to touch as much as possible. The job of the counselor is to arrange them on the floor to allow for the maximum contact. Two pennies have contact if their edges touch.

THE QUESTIONS

1. What geometric arrangement or arrangements (if more than one cluster is desirable) allows for maximum contact?

2. What is the maximum number of contact points among the 1000 pennies?

A BEGINNING

Figure 6.16 shows four pennies arranged in three different arrangements. In (a), there are three points of contact, in (b) there are four, and in (c) there are five. The maximum number of contact points for four pennies is five.

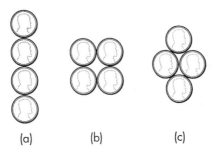

(a)   (b)   (c)

Fig. 6.16

17. Marriage Counseling for the Natural Numbers

Natural numbers often make mistakes when pairing up. But that is what counselors are for. Through a series of counseling sessions, our counselor can guarantee a reconciliation between even the most incompatible pair of natural numbers. The sessions involve the Euclidean algorithm—a time-honored method of getting to the common ground that two numbers share. This problem is one of two that analyze the acrimony that can exist between numbers. The other problem, "Conflict among the Natural Numbers" in chapter 8, explores the broader sociological effects of conflict.

THE QUESTIONS

1. If two natural numbers are 50 or less, what is the number of sessions necessary to reconcile the most incompatible pair?

2. Which pair(s) of numbers is (are) most incompatible?

3. Characterize the pairs of numbers that require just—

   a) one visit;

   b) two visits;

   c) three visits.

4. What is the smallest pair of numbers that require ten sessions?

A BEGINNING

The purpose of the counseling sessions is to discover the areas of common interest and find the greatest common ground (also known as the greatest common factor) that the numbers share. This is how the counselor operates with the numbers 10 and 36:

Session 1. It is suggested that the smaller number 10 might be a common factor. Naturally, 10 can divide 10, but when 10 is divided into 36, it leaves a remainder of 6.

Session 2. Continuing from the last session, the counselor tries the number 6 as a common factor, but when 6 is divided into 10, a remainder of 4 results.

Session 3. Picking up the number 4 from the previous session, divide 4 into 6 (not into 10 or into 36), the divisor of the previous session. This division yields a remainder of 2.

Session 4. The number 2 is now divided into 4, and the procedure leaves a remainder of 0; that means 2 divides 4 evenly. This is our last session. The greatest common factor has been found, and it is 2.

It took four sessions to uncover the greatest common factor of these two numbers. The more incompatible the two numbers are, the more sessions it takes to uncover their greatest common factor.

18. Don't Waste the Missiles

An enemy power has 100 silos, a few of which store missiles with live nuclear warheads. The others are empty shells. Our job is to figure out how many missiles we would need to fire to have a reasonable chance of disabling the loaded silos. We assume that every missile we shoot will hit its intended target. If there were only one live warhead, common sense would tell us that if 50 missiles were fired, we would have an even chance of hitting the right silo. But with two or three warheads, common sense is not so helpful. There are several possibilities: you might get lucky and hit them all right away, or you might not hit the last warhead until the 100th missile. We will approach the problem by accounting for all the scenarios and calculating an average outcome.

THE QUESTIONS

On average, how many missiles should we expect to fire to knock out the live warheads if—

1. there is one warhead?
2. there are two warheads?
3. there are three warheads?
4. there are four warheads, and we want to disable two of them?

A BEGINNING

These questions ask for the average answer of thousands of different scenarios.

Here are all the scenarios for five silos and two warheads. Let e stand for empty, w for warhead. Each grouping is a sequence of targets. The number above the combination is the number of missiles that must be fired to hit both warheads.

5	4	3	2
eeeww	eeww(e)	eww(ee)	ww(eee)
eewew	ewew(e)	wew(ee)	
eweew	weew(e)		
weeew			

The average of these ten scenarios is

$$\frac{4(5) + 3(4) + 2(3) + 1(2)}{10} = 4.$$

So, on average, it will take four missiles to knock out both warheads if there are five silos.

19. The Perfect Shuffle

Only card sharks can perform a perfect shuffle with any regularity. Average people even have considerable trouble cutting a deck into two equal piles of twenty-six cards apiece. A perfect shuffle weaves together two equal piles so that every adjacent pair of cards from one pile becomes separated by one card from the other pile. There are two different perfect shuffles—one beginning with the right-hand pile and one with the left-hand pile. We shall call them shuffle A and shuffle B. If you shuffle the cards perfectly over and over again, you will eventually return the deck to its original order. The number of shuffles that this process takes is called the *shuffle index* for that deck.

THE QUESTIONS

1. What is the shuffle A index for a deck of fifty-two cards?

2. What is the shuffle B index for a deck of fifty-two cards?

3. If you allow a combination of both kinds of shuffling, how many different orderings of the possible 52! permutations can you obtain?

4. Suppose that you have a deck of fewer than fifty-two cards. What size deck has the maximum shuffle A index? The maximum shuffle B index?

A BEGINNING

Suppose that our deck has six cards numbered 1, 2, 3, 4, 5, and 6, and they are arranged in that order from top to bottom. We denote this deck: 1 2 3 4 5 6. We denote a cut of the deck like this: 1 2 3/4 5 6. A shuffle A will begin with the right-hand pile, 4 5 6. First the 6 (the bottom card) is released, remaining on the bottom; then the 3 from the left-hand pile and the 5 and so on until the 1 is released. It remains on the top. This interweaving of the deck leaves the cards like this: 1 4 2 5 3 6. Cutting again, we get 1 4 2/5 3 6. Shuffling A again obtains 1 5 4 3 2 6. Proceeding like this gives us 1 3 5 2 4 6, then 1 2 3 4 5 6, the original ordering. We see that four shuffles restore the deck to its original order. So the shuffle A index of the deck of six cards is 4.

Shuffle B begins with the left-hand pile, 1 2 3. The 3 goes on the bottom, followed by the 6, the 2, the 5, and so on. The new top card is the 4. The series of shuffles beginning with 1 2 3 4 5 6, successively yields 4 1 5 2 6 3, 2 4 6 1 3 5, and 1 2 3 4 5 6. It takes three shuffles to restore the order; so we say that the shuffle B index for six cards is 3.

If we consider combinations of the two types of shuffles, we can get other orderings of the cards. For example, 1 2 3 4 5 6 → A → 1 4 2 5 3 6 → B → 5 1 3 4 6 2. The ordering 5 1 3 4 6 2 is not among those listed above.

20. Making Triangles out of Sausage Links

If you ever get your hands on a string of sausage links, you must try to form as many triangles as you can with them. Since the vertices of the triangle can occur only at the points where the string joins two links, the problem of how many triangles you can form is the porcine equivalent of a very nice mathematical problem: how many triangles are there with integer sides that have a fixed perimeter?

THE QUESTIONS

Suppose we have a string of 1 million links of sausage.

1. How many differently shaped triangles can be formed?

2. Of these triangles, how many are—
   a) equilateral?
   b) isosceles?
   c) scalene?

3. What is the fewest number of links necessary to be able to form at least 1 million—

   a) triangles?
   b) isosceles triangles?
   c) scalene triangles?

A BEGINNING

Figure 6.17 shows the three triangles that can be formed from a chain of nine sausages. Of these, one is equilateral, one is isosceles, and one is scalene.

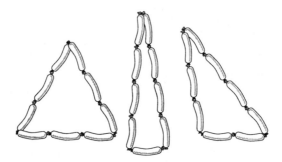

Fig. 6.17

7

**TWENTY
MATHEMATICAL
EXPEDITIONS**

21. The Genealogy of Natural Numbers

Natural numbers, like people, have family trees. Generally speaking, the smaller numbers are the older numbers, and the larger ones are the younger numbers. Specifically, if the number a divides the number b evenly, then a is said to be an *ancestor* of b, and b is a *descendant* of a. In this genealogy, the number 1 becomes the ancestor of all numbers. We shall exclude it from our population and simply think of it as some sort of supreme being.

THE QUESTIONS

1. In the population of the first trillion numbers, the number 2 has the most descendants (500 billion minus 1).

   a) Which number has the most ancestors, and how many does it have?

   b) Which number has the most relatives? (Two numbers are related if they share a common ancestor.)

2. *a*) What is the smallest number that has more than 10 000 ancestors?

   b) What is the smallest number that has more than 10 000 (smaller) relatives?

3. What is the average number of ancestors per number in the population of numbers—

   a) less than or equal to 100?

   b) less than or equal to 1000?

   c) less than or equal to 10 000?

79

4. Answer the questions in 3 for the average number of descendants per number in the population.

5. Answer the questions in 3 for the average number of relatives per number in the population.

6. *a*) Estimate the average number of ancestors per number among the population of the first trillion numbers.

b) Can a population ever be big enough to have the average number of ancestors exceed 100? If so, about how large would the population be?

7. There is an old saying among the natural numbers: "Be nice, most numbers are your kin." It is understood that old sayings should not be taken literally. After all, if you are an odd number, it could not possibly be true for you. Nevertheless, it was a shock when someone announced that if two numbers happen to meet, the chances that they are related are less than 2 in 5. Is this a fact?

A BEGINNING

You should begin by reading about the rectangular personalities of a number in chapter 4. This is a good introduction to questions 1 and 2.

Let us look at the population of the first nine numbers (we excluded 1). We can list the number of their ancestors, descendants, and relatives easily:

Number	2	3	4	5	6	7	8	9	10
Number of ancestors	0	0	1	0	2	0	2	1	2
Number of descendants	4	2	1	1	0	0	0	0	0
Number of relatives	4	2	4	1	6	0	4	2	5

Counting up the ancestors, we get 8; the descendants, 8; and the relatives, 28. That makes an average of 0.89 ancestors, 0.89 descendants, and 3.1 relatives per number.

If two numbers happen to meet, the chances that they are related can be calculated this way: Let the numbers be a and b where $a < b$. If $a = 2$, b can be one of eight numbers, four of which are related to 2: 4, 6, 8, and 10. Table 7.1 completes this study. So in this population, the chances are 14/36 = .3889 that, on a chance meeting, two numbers will be related. This bears out the announcement that the probability is less than 40 percent, but this is only a small population, and four of the nine numbers are primes.

Table 7.1
Chances that two numbers are related

a	Number of possibilities	Numbers that are related
2	8	4
3	7	2
4	6	3
5	5	1
6	4	3
7	3	0
8	2	1
9	1	0
	36	14

22. World Records
for Triangles on a Geoboard

On a geoboard with 100 pegs on a side, millions of triangles can be formed, but only a few have the distinction of holding a record. Your job, should you choose to accept it, is to find the record and the record holders for the events listed below. Note that we distinguish between two triangles only if they are not congruent; so there will be multiple record holders if at least two noncongruent triangles have tied for a record.

THE QUESTIONS

You have a square geoboard with 100 pegs on a side.

1. Area. What is the maximum area of a triangle formed on this geoboard? How many triangles hold the record? What is the minimum area? How many triangles hold this record?

2. Perimeter. What is the maximum perimeter of a triangle? How many triangles hold this record? What is the minimum perimeter? How many hold this record?

3. Interior pegs. What is the maximum number of interior pegs in a triangle? How many triangles hold the record?

4. No interior pegs. What is the maximum area of a triangle with no interior pegs? What is the maximum perimeter of a triangle with no interior pegs?

5. Boundary pegs. What is the maximum number of boundary pegs on a triangle? How many triangles hold the record?

6. No boundary pegs. What is the maximum area of a triangle with no boundary pegs? What is the maximum perimeter of a triangle with no boundary pegs?

7. a) Find a relationship between the number of boundary pegs, the number of interior pegs, and the area of a triangle.

b) Try to extend the relationship to the areas of polygons on a geoboard.

A BEGINNING

In figure 7.1, we have a geoboard with four pegs on a side, sixteen pegs in all. We have drawn a triangle that has the following characteristics:

area: 3
perimeter: $3 + 2\sqrt{2} + \sqrt{5} = 8.0645$

interior pegs: 1 (labeled a)
boundary pegs: 3 (labeled b, c, and d)

Notice that we have distinguished between vertices and boundary pegs.

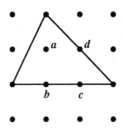

Fig. 7.1

23. Circling the Square

Three special problems in geometry date back to antiquity: the duplication of the cube, the trisection of an angle, and the squaring of a circle. The early Greek mathematicians attempted to solve these problems with straight lines and circles alone—that is, by Euclidean geometry. The third of these problems involved building the sides of a square whose area was the same as a given circle. This cannot be done with the rules of *building* that the mathematicians imposed. Here we reverse the terminology of "squaring the circle" and present a problem that *can* be solved. The solution also involves ancient mathematics—the Pythagorean theorem.

THE QUESTIONS

Consider a square of integer lattice points (m, n) where $-100 \leq m \leq 100$ and $-100 \leq n \leq 100$. Many of these points lie on circles centered at the origin with a radius ≤ 100. (If a point lies on the circle, we shall say that the circle "contains" the point.)

1. Which circle(s) of integer radius contains the most lattice points? How many lattice points are contained?

2. Which circle(s) of any radius contains the most lattice points? How many points are contained?

3. Characterize the integers that are the radii of circles that contain at least one lattice point. Characterize the numbers that are not integers that are radii of circles that contain at least one lattice point.

4. Suppose that R is an integer such that both R and $\sqrt{R}$ are radii of cirlces that contain lattice points. Find a relationship between the coordinates of the points on the two circles.

A related problem concerns the difficulty of creating the image of a circle on a screen where images are produced by lighted pixels that are arranged in a square matrix.

5. How many pixels, arranged in a square array, are necessary to create the image of a circle that contains at least 1000 points of light?

A BEGINNING

Figure 7.2 is a square made up of forty-nine lattice points (m, n) where $-3 \leq m \leq 3$ and $-3 \leq n \leq 3$. As you can see, the circle of radius $\sqrt{5}$ contains the most points, eight. The points are arranged at these positions: $(\pm 2, \pm 1)$ and $(\pm 1, \pm 2)$. The circles of integral radius 1, 2, and 3 all contain four points.

Notice that if the forty-nine dots above are light-producing pixels, then the best *circle* that can be produced contains eight points. You should check that a matrix of 121 pixels can do better—it can create a "circle" with twelve points.

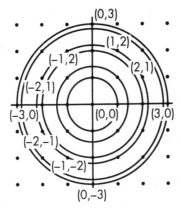

Fig. 7.2

24. The Check Is in the Mail

A confused secretary stuffs twelve checks into twelve envelopes and seals them. Then he realizes that he paid absolutely no attention to which check went into which envelope. Nevertheless, he goes ahead and mails them because he was a mathematics major; so he knows that the chances are good that no one will ever find out about his foolish lapse.

THE QUESTIONS

1. What is the probability that no check is in its correct envelope?

2. What is the probability that—

   a) exactly one check is in its correct envelope?

   b) exactly two checks are placed correctly?

   c) exactly three checks are placed correctly?

3. On average, how many checks are in correct envelopes?

4. During the stuffing process, what percentage of the checks, on average, is wrongly placed before a correct placement is made?

A BEGINNING

If the envelopes are stuffed at random, it means that any of a number of possibilities are equally likely. For example, suppose we have three checks, *a*, *b*, and *c*, and three envelopes, *A*, *B*, and *C*, where *a* belongs to *A*, *b* to *B*, and *c* to *C*. We have six possible match-ups:

1) *aA, bB, cC*	4) *aB, bC, cA*
2) *aA, bC, cB*	5) *aC, bA, cB*
3) *aB, bA, cC*	6) *aC, bB, cA*

Numbers 4 and 5 have no matches, numbers 2, 3, and 6 each have one match, and number 1 has three matches. Thus the probability that none are matched correctly is 2/6 = 1/3, that one is correct is 1/2, and that three are correct is 1/6. Of the six possibilities, the total number of correct matches is six; so, on average, there is 6/6, or 1, match per mailing.

Assuming that the order of stuffing proceeds as indicated (and this is as good an assumption as any), we see that the number of checks that are wrongly placed before a correct match is made is, respectively, 0, 0, 2, 3, 3, 1. This adds up to nine in six possibilities, or 1.5 per mailing. Since there are three envelopes in this example, we can conclude that, on average, 50 percent of the placements are wrong before one is correct.

25. Squares within Squares and Cubes within Cubes

In chapter 4, we discussed the many rectangular personalities of a number. The question was raised about how many squares can be drawn within a square matrix of dots. If you make a square of dots, take a pencil, and start drawing in the squares, you will find that the answer is a lot—more than you might suspect. A natural extension of this problem is to count the number of cubic lattices that can be formed by joining dots arranged in a cubic matrix. Since it is difficult to draw a cubic matrix, joining dots with a pencil doesn't work very well unless you are gifted with exceptional spatial intuition.

THE QUESTIONS

Suppose that we have 10 000 dots arrayed neatly in a square 100 dots on a side.

1. How many different sizes of squares can be formed by joining dots?

2. How many different squares can be formed by joining dots?

Suppose that we have 1 million dots arranged in a cube 100 dots on a side.

3. How many different sizes of cubes can be formed by joining the dots?

4. How many different cubes can be formed by joining dots?

A BEGINNING

In figure 7.3, there are sixteen dots arrayed in a square. There are obvious squares that are oriented horizontally and vertically. However, there are also

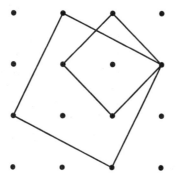

Fig. 7.3

squares of a slanted persuasion. We have drawn two of these. The smaller has area 2, the larger, area 5.

The chart below counts the number of squares of different sizes. By *size* we mean the area.

Size of square (area)	1	4	9	2	5
Number of squares	9	4	1	4	2

This chart shows that there are five different sizes of squares, and there are twenty different squares that can be formed by joining dots.

Figure 7.4 shows a cube with twenty-seven dots, three dots on a side. The chart below lists the number of different cubes of different sizes. Here, size means volume.

Size of cube (volume)	1	8
Number of cubes	8	1

So, there are two different sizes of cubes and nine different cubes that can be formed by joining dots.

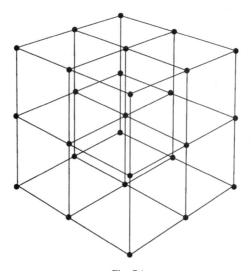

Fig. 7.4

26. Triangles within Triangles

Like "Squares within Squares," this question can be approached by simply taking a pencil and connecting dots. The background is a matrix of dots in the shape of an equilateral triangle. The dots that you connect should also form an equilateral triangle. The questions in this problem vary as much in difficulty as any problem in the book. Questions 1 and 2 are pleasant excursions; questions 4 and 5 are tricky expeditions.

THE QUESTIONS

An array of dots is shaped like an equilateral triangle that is 100 levels deep.

1. How many unit triangles can be formed by connecting dots?

2. How many right-side-up equilateral triangles can be formed by connecting dots?

3. How many equilateral triangles, right side up or upside down, can be formed?

4. How many different sizes of equilateral triangles of any orientation can be formed?

5. In all, how many equilateral triangles can be formed?

A BEGINNING

Figure 7.5 has four levels of dots arranged in an equilateral triangle. Counting, we see that there are six unit, right-side-up, equilateral triangles and three unit, upside-down, equilateral triangles, making nine unit triangles in all.

Continuing counting, we find three right-side-up triangles of the next larger size and one of the largest size (the whole triangle). This makes ten total right-side-up triangles. There are no upside-down triangles larger than the three unit ones that we already found. So there are thirteen equilateral triangles in all that are either right side up or upside down.

Figure 7.6 shows two more triangles in the figure that are oriented differently. This makes a grand total of fifteen equilateral triangles in all. The fifteen triangles are of four different sizes. In the table below we distinguish the size by the side. Let the side of the unit triangle be 1.

Size (length of side)	1	2	3	$\sqrt{3}$
Number of triangles	9	3	1	2

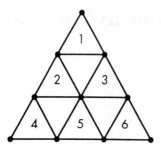

Fig. 7.5

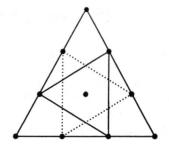

Fig. 7.6

27. The First One to the Origin Wins

This game is played on the integral lattice points in the first quadrant. Two players play the game. It begins at the point (m, n), and the players take turns moving toward the origin. They may move in one of three directions: horizontally toward the y-axis, vertically toward the x-axis, or along a 45° diagonal down and to the left. They may move in any of these directions as far as they like. The first one to the origin wins.

THE QUESTIONS

1. If the starting point is (79, 122), which player will win the game, the player that moves first or the one that moves second? Explain the strategy of the winner.

2. How many special points (m, n) are there if m and n are less than or equal to 1000?

3. If you plot the special points, they lie roughly on two straight lines that pass through the origin. What can you say about the slopes of the lines?

A BEGINNING

Figure 7.7 is a sample game beginning at the point (4, 3). The first player moves diagonally down to the point (2, 1) and stops. The second player surveys the situation and realizes he has lost. He may move down to (2, 0), left to (1, 1) or (0, 1), or diagonally down to (1, 0). All these stopping places are on a direct path to the origin. Points like (2, 1) represent guaranteed wins for the player who can reach them (assuming he knows how to play the game) and guaranteed losses for the player who must play from them. We call such points *special points*.

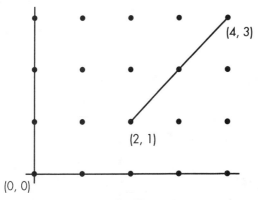

Fig. 7.7

28. Mathematics and String Art

Ninety-nine nails are arranged around the outside of a circular board, and every nail is connected to every other nail by a stretched string. A nice visual pattern is formed showing many string crossings and many tiny regions surrounded by strings. A hundredth nail is pounded into the board, and new strings are added to connect the new nail to the other ninety-nine.

THE QUESTIONS

1. How many new string crossings have been added?

2. How many new regions have resulted?

3. How many string crossings are there now with 100 nails on the board?

4. How many regions are there on the board with 100 nails?

A BEGINNING

Suppose that we have five nails on a board numbered 1 through 5, and we add a sixth nail between 5 and 1 as pictured in figure 7.8.

The string joining 6 to 1 adds no new crossings and one new region. The string from 6 to 2 adds three new crossings and four new regions. The chart below displays the new crossings and new regions.

Joinings	6-1	6-2	6-3	6-4	6-5	Total
New crossings	0	3	4	3	0	10
New regions	1	4	5	4	1	15

The board with 6 nails has fifteen string crossings and thirty-one regions. Notice that the 6 nails must be arranged so that the maximum number of crossings and regions is obtained. Thus, figure 7.9, showing three strings meeting in the center, is not allowed. This constraint applies to the 100-nail string art as well; we want the maximum number of crossings and regions.

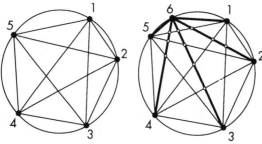

Fig. 7.8   Fig. 7.9

29. You Can't See the Forest for the Trees

You are in the middle of a perfect orchard. The centers of the trees are equally spaced one unit apart along vertical and horizontal lines, and all the trunks are circular with the same radius. It is a truly beautiful sight.

THE QUESTIONS

The orchard covers 40 000 square units.

1. If the radius of the trees is 0—

   a) how many trees are obscured from your view?

   b) which pair (or pairs) of trees appears closest together?

   c) which pair (or pairs) appears farthest apart?

2. How big must the radius of the tree trunks be so that you cannot see out of the orchard in any direction?

3. If the tree trunks are of the radius in question 2, are any of the trees, formerly visible in question 1, now completely obscured? If so, how many can you find?

4. How big must the radius of the trunks be so that at least one tree, formerly visible, becomes completely obscured?

A BEGINNING

Figure 7.10 shows the centers of eighty-one trees. If we delete the tree in the middle so that we can stand there, there are eighty trees in all. The area of this orchard is sixty-four square units.

Putting the orchard on a coordinate graph, we have the centers of the trees located at the lattice points (x, y) where $-4 \leq x \leq 4$, $-4 \leq y \leq 4$. The observer is at the origin.

Obviously, if the dots had a radius of 1/2, the view from the origin would be obscured in every direction and all you would see would be four large trees centered at $(1, 0)$, $(-1, 0)$, $(0, 1)$, and $(0, -1)$. But the radius would not have to be this large to obstruct our view to the outside. In fact, a radius of 1/4 would be sufficient to totally obstruct our view. To test this statement, we may begin like this:

Stand at the origin looking east. What you see is the tree centered at $(1, 0)$. Turn counterclockwise until you see the next tree; it is centered at $(4, 1)$. Now using analytic geometry, you can find the line tangent to the trunk of the tree centered at $(1, 0)$ and passing through the origin. This is your line of sight. You will find that this line hits the trunk of the tree centered at (4, 1). An easier way of proceeding is to check that the line $y = (1/5)x$ intersects both trunks. This insures that the trunk of the tree at (1, 0) partially obscures the trunk of the tree at (4, 1), and so there is no space between the trunks to see out of the orchard.

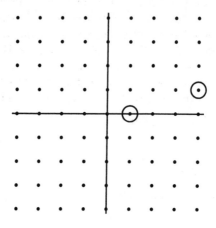

Fig. 7.10

30. A Population Explosion of Rational Numbers

My town is located on the real line. The city limits are 0 and 1. I am the oldest citizen. I am 1/2. A few years ago we were happy. Our town was a nice size; it contained all the fractions with denominators less than or equal to 50. Now we are told that things will be changing. Beginning next month new numbers will be moving in; first the numbers with denominator 51 (there are thirty-two of them); then, the following month, the numbers with denominator 52 (there are twenty-four of these). And it will continue this way for who knows how long.

I wonder—

THE QUESTIONS

1. When will the town—

    a) double in population?

    b) triple in population?

    c) quadruple in population?

2. After the numbers with denominator 100 arrive—

    a) how big will the town be?

    b) how many will be males?

    c) how close will the closest neighbors be?

    d) how many of the new numbers will move into my neighborhood? Into my good friend 1/3's neighborhood?

3. Could the population ever reach 1 million?

    a) If it did, when would it happen?

    b) What would the percent of males in the population be then?

    c) Will it happen in my lifetime?

A BEGINNING

Figure 7.11 shows a town of numbers with denominators 8 or less. The numbers live on the line in their natural order, but the spacing between the numbers is not accurate in the figure. The population numbers twenty-one. A male number has both an odd and an even part (rather like chromosomes). Female numbers are odd in both the numerator and the denominator. Fifteen of our twenty-one numbers are male. The neighborhood around 1/2 extends from 3/7 to 4/7, the two nearest neighbors of 1/2. When the town contained only fractions of denominator 5 or less, the neighborhood of 1/2 extended from 2/5 to 3/5, but since then, 3/7 and 4/7 have moved in.

0 (——————————————————————————————————————) 1

$\frac{1}{8}$ $\frac{1}{7}$ $\frac{1}{6}$ $\frac{1}{5}$ $\frac{1}{4}$ $\frac{2}{7}$ $\frac{1}{3}$ $\frac{3}{8}$ $\frac{2}{5}$ $\frac{3}{7}$ $\frac{1}{2}$ $\frac{4}{7}$ $\frac{3}{5}$ $\frac{5}{8}$ $\frac{2}{3}$ $\frac{5}{7}$ $\frac{3}{4}$ $\frac{4}{5}$ $\frac{5}{6}$ $\frac{6}{7}$ $\frac{7}{8}$

Fig. 7.11

31. A Population Explosion on the Rational Circle

This problem follows "A Population Explosion of Rational Numbers." As the population of rationals increases along the segment $(0, 1)$, the numbers naturally decide to buy second homes for vacation purposes. The unit circle (see fig. 7.12) is an ideal resort area. Locations there have rational coordinates (r, s) where $r^2 + s^2 = 1$. The rational number P on the line segment buys a plot on the circle from a real estate agent who lives at the point $(0, -1)$ on the unit circle. The plot that is sold to point P is the point L on the circle that lies on the line joining the agent to the buyer. These plots are all in the first quadrant.

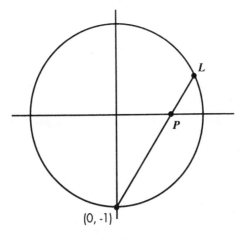

Fig. 7.12

THE QUESTIONS

1. How many resort plots are there on the circle located at coordinates with denominators 100 or less? List the owners by gender—male and female. (As in problem 30, male numbers have both an odd and an even part and female numbers have an odd numerator and an odd denominator.)

2. The plots (r, s) and (s, r) are symmetric. Find a relationship between the two numbers on the line that own symmetric plots. What can you say about the gender of the owners?

3. Suppose the line segment is populated by numbers with denominator 100 or less.

   a) What is the largest denominator of the plots owned?

b) How many of the numbers own resort plots with coordinates of denominator 10 000 or less?

c) How many of these owners are male?

d) Which male and female own plots that are closest together?

4. All the plots on the circle with denominators less than 1 million have been prepared for sale.

a) Approximately how many plots have been prepared?

b) These plots will eventually be bought by townspeople.
What will the population of the town be when—

(1) the last location is bought?

(2) the last male-owned location is bought?

5. If the town extends its right-hand city limit from 1 to $\sqrt{2}$, a new circle of resort locations may be opened on the circle $x^2 + y^2 = 2$. In fact, in the not too distant future, further expansion may call for extending the city limit to $\sqrt{3}$ and opening the circle $x^2 + y^2 = 3$.

a) Analyze the situation for rational points on the circle of radius $\sqrt{2}$ as you did for the unit circle. Clearly, the point (1, 1) is on the circle. Are there any more?

b) Do a similar analysis for the circle of radius $\sqrt{3}$.

A BEGINNING

Suppose that the line segment is populated by the numbers with denominators 3 or less, namely, 1/2, 1/3, and 2/3. The homes assigned to these points are located at (4/5, 3/5), (3/5, 4/5), and (12/13, 5/13), respectively. We can show this by simply extending a line from the point (0, −1) to *P* on the line as shown in the figure. The intersection of this line with the unit circle gives the plot location, *L*.

Thus for denominators 3 or less, the largest denominator of a coordinate of a resort plot is 13. The points 1/2 and 1/3 have symmetric plots. There are two plots with denominators 5 or less (unless you can find more).

32. A Cheap Ruler

When I was shopping for my back-to-school supplies, I saw a strange bargain: "Buy a defective ruler and a defective protractor for the price of a regular nondefective ruler." The defective ruler was a foot long like the regular one, but instead of having 11 marks designating the inches between the ends of the ruler, it had only 4 marks that were not evenly spaced. The defective protractor did not have the 360 marks designating the degrees as on a standard circular protractor. Instead, it had fewer than 50 marks, and they, too, were unevenly spaced. Nevertheless, the bargain was too good to pass up, so I took it. Only later did I learn just how good it really was. You see, these so-called defective instruments can, in fact, measure just as accurately as their nondefective counterparts.

THE QUESTIONS

1. On a measuring stick, what is the minimum number of marks needed to measure accurately to within—

   a) 1 inch on a yardstick?

   b) 1 centimeter on a meterstick?

   c) 1/32 inch on a foot-long ruler?

2. On a measuring stick, what is the maximum accuracy you can attain if you use—

   a) 5 marks? 6 marks? 7 marks? 10 marks?

   b)100 marks?

3. On a protractor, what is the minimum number of marks needed if you want to measure accurately to within—

   a) 10 degrees?

   b) 1 degree?

4. On a protractor, what is the maximum accuracy you can attain if you use—

   a) 4 marks? 5 marks? 6 marks?

   b) 7 marks?

5. Find as many perfect markings as you can.

A BEGINNING

Let us look at the defective ruler with 4 marks (fig. 7.13). This ruler with these markings can measure exactly any of the eleven distances between 0 and 12 inches; that is, it can measure accurately to within 1/12 the length of the ruler.

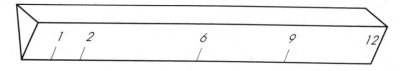

Fig. 7.13

Mark	Measure	Mark	Measure	Mark	Measure
0 to 1,	1 inch	1 to 6,	5 inches	0 to 9,	9 inches
0 to 2,	2 inches	0 to 6,	6 inches	2 to 12,	10 inches
9 to 12,	3 inches	2 to 9,	7 inches	1 to 12,	11 inches
2 to 6,	4 inches	1 to 9,	8 inches		

Actually, 4 marks allow us to measure a stick accurately to within 1/13 its length. Look at the ruler in figure 7.14 where the unit length is 1/13. We can get all twelve different lengths using the marks like this:

0 to 1 (or 1 to 2)	6 to 13
0 to 2	2 to 10
10 to 13	1 to 10
2 to 6 (or 6 to 10)	0 to 10
1 to 6	2 to 13
0 to 6	1 to 13

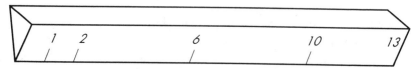

Fig. 7.14

Notice that two of the lengths, the first and the fourth, can be measured in two different ways.

This is the maximum accuracy we can obtain with 4 marks. Try as you might, you cannot split a stick into fourteen equal pieces and measure all thirteen of its fractional lengths using an arrangement of only 4 marks. We should note that, theoretically, the maximum precision could not exceed accuracy to within 1/15 the length of the stick. This is because there are fifteen distances that can be measured between pairs of marks (and marks and endpoints) if we have 4 marks between the two endpoints. Of course, as we saw above, not all these distances are distinct.

On a circular protractor, suppose we want to measure an angle to within 60° accuracy; that is, to within 1/6 the full angle measure of the circle. As we see in figure 7.15, we do not need to mark six different positions on the circle (0, 1, 2, 3, 4, 5); only three are necessary: 0, 1, and 4. Measuring clockwise, we see that 0 to 1, 4 to 0, 1 to 4 (and 4 to 1), 0 to 4, and 1 to 0 get all five measurements.

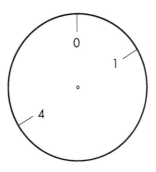

Fig. 7.15

Actually, the proper three marks can yield measurements with accuracy to within 1/7 the measure of the circle. Using the protractor in figure 7.16, we can get the six measurements like this: 0 to 1, 1 to 3, 0 to 3, 3 to 0, 3 to 1, and 1 to 0. Notice that every measurement is achieved in exactly one way. Therefore, accuracy to within 1/7 is clearly the maximum accuracy we can achieve with three marks.

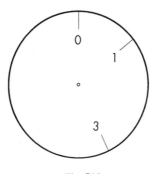

Fig. 7.16

When a marking, like the one above, yields the ideal situation, that is, all possible measurements are achieved in a unique way, then the marking is called a *perfect marking*.

33. Balance Scales
Expose Counterfeit Coin

Our mission is to find the single counterfeit coin in a pile of coins. It looks the same as the real coins, but it has a different weight. We do not know if it is lighter or heavier, and we must find that out.

We are allowed to use only balance scales, but we may use them as many times as necessary to uncover the counterfeit coin and determine its relative weight.

THE QUESTIONS

1. If we use the scales only three times, what is the maximum number of coins we can sift through to discover the counterfeit one and determine its relative weight?

2. If we have 1000 coins in our pile, what is the minimum number of weighings on our scales that would be sufficient to discover the counterfeit coin and determine its relative weight?

A BEGINNING

Suppose we have five coins in our pile, labeled a, b, c, d, and e. We use the following notation to help in our explanation: $ab < cd$ means that the two coins a and b together are lighter than the two coins c and d together.

First weighing. We weigh ab against cd. Here are the possible outcomes:

$$ab < cd, \ ab = cd, \ cd < ab$$

Now if $ab = cd$, then we know immediately that e is the counterfeit coin. To find its relative weight, we can weigh it against a good coin, say a. The outcome of that weighing will complete the problem.

If $ab < cd$, we continue like this:

Second weighing. Since we know that e is good, we weigh it against a. Here are the possible outcomes:

$$a < e \text{ and } a = e$$

(We know that $e < a$ is impossible because $ab < cd$.)

Suppose that $a < e$. Then we know that a is counterfeit and lighter.

Suppose that $a = e$. Then we know that one of three things is possible. Either b is light, or c or d is heavy.

Third weighing. Weigh c against d. The possible outcomes are these:

$$c < d, \ d < c, \text{ or } c = d$$

If $c < d$, then d is counterfeit and heavy; if $d < c$, then c is counterfeit and heavy; if $c = d$, then b is counterfeit and light.

So three weighings have completed the task—almost. We must examine the possibility that $cd < ab$, a possibility that we neglected at the beginning of our quest. It is sufficient to say that the procedure for this possibility is analogous to the one we did for $ab < cd$.

In conclusion, if we have five coins, two weighings are not sufficient to determine the counterfeit coin; three weighings are sufficient.

34. Building Numbers the Egyptian Way

The Egyptians were fond of building fractions out of unit fractions. Since any fraction, a/b, is the sum of unit fractions, $1/b + 1/b + \ldots + 1/b$ (a times), it is clear that this is possible. But the challenge that the Egyptian mathematicians set for themselves was to express a fraction as the sum of the fewest unit fractions. In this study, we shall restrict ourselves to proper fractions that have been reduced to lowest terms.

THE QUESTIONS

1. Find the fraction with smallest denominator that cannot be built by fewer than—

   a) three unit fractions;

   b) four unit fractions;

   c) five unit fractions;

   d) ten unit fractions.

2. Which fraction or fractions, a/b, need the most unit fraction building blocks if b is less than or equal to—

   a) 50?

   b) 100?

3. Clearly, every fraction with numerator 2 or less can be built by at most two unit fractions. Fill in the blanks of these ancient Egyptian theorems:

   a) Every fraction with numerator _____ or less can be built by at most three unit fractions.

   b) Every fraction with numerator _____ or less can be built by at most four unit fractions.

   c) Every fraction with numerator _____ or less can be built by at most five unit fractions.

4. Would the answers to questions 1, 2, and 3 change if—

   a) we insisted that the unit fraction building blocks all be of different size? If so, how?

   b) we allowed subtraction as well as addition of unit fractions in our building process? If so, how?

A BEGINNING

Let us build the fraction 3/8 out of unit fractions. The simplest way is

$$3/8 = 1/8 + 1/8 + 1/8.$$

But in fact, there are several ways that 3/8 can be written. For example:

$$3/8 = 1/3 + 1/24$$
$$= 1/4 + 1/8$$
$$= 1/5 + 1/8 + 1/20$$
$$= 1/6 + 1/8 + 1/12$$

Our concern here is the fact that two unit fractions are sufficient to do the building job.

35. Pool with Real Pockets

In the excursion "Pool, Anyone?" in chapter 6, we examined the path of a "ball" on a pool table with no pockets. The path of the ball came to an end only when the ball hit a corner of the table exactly. If we have small-sized pockets on the table, the ball can end its path in a pocket without an exact corner hit. This is more like real pool.

In this problem, the dimensions of the table are such that it is impossible for a ball to enter a corner exactly (assuming that we shoot the ball at a 45° angle from the lower left corner). So on this table, the path of the ball can come to an end only if there are pockets with size. Naturally, the length of the path and the number of bounces of the ball will depend on the size of the pockets.

THE QUESTIONS

Suppose our pool table measures 1 by $\sqrt{2}$, and we shoot the ball at a 45° angle from the lower left corner.

1. If the size of the pocket is 1/10, how many bounces will the ball take and into which pocket will it fall?

2. Answer question 1 for a pocket size of 1/10 000.

3. The size of the pocket determines the path of the ball, its bounces, and its exit pocket. As the size of the pocket varies, what can you say about—

   a) the number of bounces that are possible?

   b) the different pockets into which the ball can fall?

   c) the range of pocket sizes that will leave the path unchanged?

4. How small must the pockets be to insure that the ball will bounce at least 1 million times before falling into one?

5. If the pockets are larger than your answer to question 4, what is the maximum number of bounces that a ball can take before entering a pocket?

A BEGINNING

The pocket is shaped like an isosceles triangle with its vertex at the corner of the table. The size of a pocket is the length of one side of the triangle. See figure 7.17. Suppose the pocket has size 1/4. The path of the ball is shown in the figure. It takes one bounce at the top of the table at point A, a distance of $\sqrt{2} - 1$ from the upper right corner. The ball then heads toward point B, which is $\sqrt{2} - 1$ below the corner and $2 - \sqrt{2} = 0.5858$ above the lower right corner. After bouncing at B, it goes toward the bottom of the table and point C. Point C is also 0.5858 from the lower right corner. The ball then heads up toward point D, which is $3 - 2\sqrt{2} = 0.1716$ below the upper left corner. Since the pocket protrudes 0.25 from the corner, the ball is caught in that pocket. Notice that if the pockets had been of size 1/3 or 1/5, the path would have been the same: three bounces and ending in the upper left corner. In fact, the range of pocket size for this path of three bounces is $3 - 2\sqrt{2}$ (0.1716) to $|1 - \sqrt{2}|$ (0.4142). If the pocket had been larger than $|1 - \sqrt{2}|$, the ball would have gone into the upper right corner without any bounces at all.

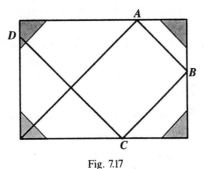

Fig. 7.17

36. Sightings of the Rare Primitive Pythagorean Triangle

We have already studied triangles with integral sides in the problem "Making Triangles out of Sausage Links" in chapter 6. There we split the triangles into three categories: scalene, isosceles, and equilateral. Another exploration, "Making Triangles out of Straws" in chapter 8, splits triangles into two categories: acute and obtuse. The rare and special triangles, however, are the right triangles, and the especially special theorem that relates the sides of the right triangle is the Pythagorean theorem. Everyone knows, or ought to know, what it says: If the lengths of the shorter sides of a right triangle (the legs) are labeled a and b and the longer one (the hypotenuse) is labeled c, then $a^2 + b^2 = c^2$. The Pythagorean triangle is a right triangle with sides of integral length. The *primitive* Pythagorean triangle is a Pythagorean triangle whose sides are relatively prime; that is, the greatest common divisor of the lengths of its three sides is 1. In the world of triangles, these triangles are rare indeed.

THE QUESTIONS

1. How many primitive triangles have sides less than or equal to 100?

2. How many primitive Pythagorean triangles have sides less than or equal to 200? To 400?

3. Estimate how many primitive Pythagorean triangles have sides less than or equal to 1 million.

4. Answer questions 1, 2, and 3 for *all* Pythagorean triangles.

To spot Pythagorean triangles, look for certain characteristics. For example, check the measurements of the legs. What can you say about these numbers? Also, the measurements of the hypotenuse are distinctive. What can you say about the areas of Pythagorean triangles? Comment on the truth of the following sayings:

5. If the triangle is Pythagorean, then—

   a) the length of one of its legs is divisible by 3;

   b) the length of one of its legs is divisible by 4;

   c) the length of one of its sides is divisible by 5;

   d) the product of its three sides is divisible by 60;

   e) the area is divisible by 6;

   f) if it is also primitive, any two sides are relatively prime.

Several different Pythagorean triangles can share some of the same measurements.

6. If you have sighted a leg that measures 48, how many possible Pythagorean triangles might you be looking at? How many of these are primitive?

7. What leg measurement less than or equal to 100 is shared by the most Pythagorean triangles? The most primitive triangles?

8. Answer questions 6 and 7 for hypotenuse measurements less than or equal to 100.

9. What is the smallest measurement of a side that can belong to more than 100 different possible Pythagorean triangles? Answer this also for primitive triangles.

There are no isosceles Pythagorean triangles, that is, triangles with the same leg measurement.

10. Of all the Pythagorean triangles with leg size less than or equal to 1 million, which comes closest to being isosceles?

A BEGINNING

The Pythagorean triangles are hard to find, but we can generate them with keen searching or with a computer program. The problem "A Population Explosion on the Rational Circle" also gives a way of generating them. That particular exploration can also lend insight into other questions asked here.

Notice that if you spy a side of length 5, you may have the primitive triangle with measurements 3, 4, 5, or you may have spotted the primitive triangle 5, 12, 13. If you see a leg of length 12, you may have discovered a primitive triangle with measurements 5, 12, 13, or 12, 35, 37, or a nonprimitive one of 9, 12, 15 or 12, 16, 20.

37. Sightings of the Uncommon Heron Triangle

In the world of triangles with sides of integral length, the Heron triangle has an integral area. Heron triangles are uncommon but not as rare as the Pythagorean triangles. Heron triangles are named after Heron of Alexandria, a Greek scientist who lived during the first century A.D. and is credited with the ingenious formula relating the area of a triangle to the length of its sides:

$$A = \sqrt{s(s - a)(s - b)(s - c)}$$

Here a, b, and c stand for the length of the sides and $s = (1/2)(a + b + c)$. So s stands for half the perimeter. As with Pythagorean triangles, we will distinguish between primitive Heron triangles and nonprimitive ones. Primitive Heron triangles have side measurements whose greatest common divisor is 1.

THE QUESTIONS

1. List all the different primitive Heron triangles with area less than or equal to 100.

2. How many different primitive Heron triangles are there with sides less than or equal to 25? 50? 100?

3. Which of these triangles (in 1 and 2) is closest to being equilateral?

4. Estimate how many different primitive Heron triangles there are with sides less than or equal to 200, to 1000, to 1 million.

5. Comment on the truth of the following statements:

   a) Every Pythagorean triangle is a Heron triangle.

   b) The length of a side of a Heron triangle is even.

   c) The length of a side of a Heron triangle is a multiple of 3.

   d) The length of a side of a Heron triangle is a multiple of 5.

   e) The area of a Heron triangle is a multiple of 6.

6. It is said that every Heron triangle has at least one altitude of integral length. Is this true?

7. Triangles whose perimeter and area are the same number (and that number is an integer) are called *Moon triangles*.

   a) List all Heron triangles that are Moon triangles.

   b) Are there Moon triangles with rational sides? If so, list them.

c) Are there any other Moon triangles? If so, list them.

d) Find the smallest Moon triangle. Find the largest Moon triangle.

A BEGINNING

The Pythagorean triangle whose sides are 3, 4, and 5 is a Heron triangle. The area of this triangle is $(1/2)$ (3) (4) = 6. The triangle with sides of length 13, 14, 15 is also a Heron triangle because its area is an integer. Check it out: $A = \sqrt{21(21 - 13)(21 - 14)(21 - 15)} = \sqrt{7056} = 84$.

38. The Classic Matchup: Heads or Tails

Flipping a coin to pick a winner is a classic way of deciding an issue. Usually it takes a single coin toss to settle matters: "Heads you win, tails I win." But it can take several tosses. For example, it may take two or more tosses with the winner being the first to win two out of three tosses, or three out of five tosses, or . . . thirteen out of twenty-five tosses. We choose to concentrate most of our exploration on a variation of this game where a coin is tossed twenty-five times. We are not concerned with the winner of this game; after all, each side has an even chance of winning. Our concern is with the mathematical ebb and flow of the game. There are 2^{25} (33 554 432) different possible games that can occur, and although anything can happen, we are interested in the tendencies of the average game.

THE QUESTIONS

1. In what percentage of the games does—
    a) the winner lead throughout the game?
    b) the loser lead at least once?

2. In the average game, how many times will—
    a) the game be tied?
    b) the lead change hands?

3. In an average game, what percentage of the time will—
    a) the winner be in the lead?
    b) the loser be in the lead?

4. If the game were to end when a person got 13 heads (or 13 tails)—
    a) how long would the average game be?
    b) how many games would take the full 25 tosses?

A BEGINNING

Suppose the game were just 5 tosses long. There are 2^5 (32) possible outcomes. We will list 16 of them here; the other 16 have a symmetric behavior.

(1) HHHHH	(5) HHTHH	(9) HTHHT	(13) HTTHH
(2) HHHHT	(6) HHTHT	(10) HTHHT	(14) HTTHT
(3) HHHTH	(7) HHTTH	(11) HTHTH	(15) HTTTH
(4) HHHTT	(8) HHTTT	(12) HTHTT	(16) HTTTT

Notice that in games 1, 2, 3, 4, 5, and 6, H leads throughout. So in 6/16, or 37.5 percent, of the games, the winner leads throughout. In games 8, 12, 13, 14, 15, and 16, the loser leads at least once. That is also 37.5 percent of the games.

In games 7, 8, 9, 10, 15, and 16, there is one tie; in games 11, 12, 13, and 14, there are two ties. All in all, there are fourteen ties in 16 games. So, on average, there is 0.875, or slightly less than one, tie per game. In games 8, 12, 14, 15, and 16, there is one lead change, and in 13 there are two lead changes. This makes a total of seven lead changes in 16 games, or 0.4375 per game.

The numbers below list the number of tosses in games 1 through 16 that the winner leads followed by the number of tosses that the loser leads:

5, 0	4, 0
5, 0	4, 0
5, 0	3, 0
5, 0	1, 2
5, 0	2, 1
5, 0	2, 1
4, 0	3, 1
1, 3	3, 1

Out of the 16 games, the winner leads fifty-seven times, or 3.5625 tosses per game, or 71.25 percent of the time. The loser leads nine times, or 11.25 percent of each game. The game is tied 17.5 percent of the time.

If the game were to end when one side got three wins, then games numbered 1, 2, 3, and 4 would end after 3 tosses; games 5, 6, 9, 10, 15, and 16 would end after 4 tosses, and games 7, 8, 11, 12, 13, and 14 would go the full 5 tosses. So we have a total of $4(3) + 6(4) + 6(5) = 66$ tosses in 16 games, or an averge of 4.125 tosses per game. Since 6 of the games take all 5 tosses, that tells us that 37.5 percent of all possible games go the full distance.

39. Sharing the Candy

After a trip around the neighborhood on Halloween, we have lots of jelly beans. There are many different ways of distributing the beans among us. For example, if we have four beans, we could give one apiece to four people (we can denote this by (1, 1, 1, 1)); we could give two to one person and one to two others (2, 1, 1); we could give two apiece to two people (2, 2); we could give three to one person and one to another (3, 1); or we could give all four to one person (4). That makes a total of five different ways of sharing the jelly beans.

THE QUESTIONS

We have 100 jelly beans to distribute.

1. How many ways can this be done?

2. How many ways can this be done if all the groups are of different sizes?

3. How many ways can this be done if all groups must contain an odd number of beans?

A BEGINNING

Let us look at the problem using 10 jelly beans. The question is equivalent to finding how many ways we can add whole numbers to make 10 where the ordering of the addition is irrelevant; for example $3 + 7$ and $7 + 3$ are not distinguished as different.

We can list the different ways as in figure 7.18.

10	5, 3, 2	3, 3, 3, 1
9, 1	5, 3, 1, 1	3, 3, 2, 2
8, 2	5, 2, 2, 1	3, 3, 2, 1, 1
8, 1, 1	5, 2, 1, 1, 1	3, 3, 1, 1, 1, 1
7, 3	5, 1, 1, 1, 1, 1	3, 2, 2, 2, 1
7, 2, 1	4, 4, 2	3, 2, 2, 1, 1, 1
7, 1, 1, 1	4, 4, 1, 1	3, 2, 1, 1, 1, 1, 1
6, 4	4, 3, 3	3, 1, 1, 1, 1, 1, 1, 1
6, 3, 1	4, 3, 2, 1	2, 2, 2, 2, 2
6, 2, 2	4, 3, 1, 1, 1	2, 2, 2, 2, 1, 1
6, 2, 1, 1	4, 2, 2, 2	2, 2, 2, 1, 1, 1, 1
6, 1, 1, 1, 1	4, 2, 2, 1, 1	2, 2, 1, 1, 1, 1, 1, 1
5, 5	4, 2, 1, 1, 1, 1	2, 1, 1, 1, 1, 1, 1, 1, 1
5, 4, 1	4, 1, 1, 1, 1, 1, 1	1, 1, 1, 1, 1, 1, 1, 1, 1, 1

Fig. 7.18

There are forty-two different possibilities listed in the figure. Ten of them are underlined; they are the ones with groups of all different sizes. Let us record our findings:

Largest group	10	9	8	7	6	5	4	3	2	1	Total
Number of possibilities	1	1	2	3	5	7	9	8	5	1	42
Number of possibilities with groups of different sizes	1	1	1	2	2	2	1	0	0	0	10

If all the groups were to contain only odd numbers, we would have the following ten possibilities:

9, 1	5, 1, 1, 1, 1, 1
7, 3	3, 3, 3, 1
7, 1, 1, 1	3, 3, 1, 1, 1, 1
5, 5	3, 1, 1, 1, 1, 1, 1, 1,
5, 3, 1, 1	1, 1, 1, 1, 1, 1, 1, 1, 1, 1

40. Cutting a Diamond

You are a master gem cutter, and you are faced with the ultimate challenge. You must cut a diamond into as many different pieces as you can, but each piece must be unique, and each piece must be a perfect cut. A *perfect cut* is a cut whose size is a particular fraction of the original size—a unit fraction.

THE QUESTIONS

1. What is the maximum number of different perfect cuts into which the diamond can be split—

  a) if the pieces must be greater than or equal to 1/50?

  b) if the pieces must be greater than or equal to 1/100?

2. If your job is to get 100 different perfect cuts with the smallest cut being as large as possible, what would the size of the smallest one be?

A BEGINNING

Let us suppose that the cuts must all be greater than or equal to 1/10. The problem involves finding unit fractions of different sizes that add up to 1. For example, 1/2 + 1/3 + 1/6 = 1. In fact, these three unit fractions are the only ones that add to 1 with different denominators all less than or equal to 10. If we raise the limit from 10 to 25, we can do the job with pieces of size 1/3, 1/4, 1/6, 1/8, 1/12, and 1/24. Six cuts is not bad, but we can probably do better.

If we were asked to get four perfect cuts with the smallest being as large as possible, we would offer 1/2, 1/4, 1/6, and 1/12 as our answer. The problem "Number Building in the World of Unit Fractions" in chapter 6, can help in this problem.

8

TWENTY COMPUTER-ASSISTED EXPLORATIONS

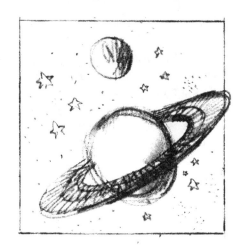

41. A March to the North Pole

We are at the final base camp just 50 miles from the North Pole. It is really cold now, and progress is slow. Each of us can carry provisions that can keep us going for 20 miles. Luckily, we can store provisions in the ice as we move along. No one of us, individually, could reach the pole, but if we work as a team in an efficient way, we can succeed.

THE QUESTIONS

1. How many people do we need to mount a successful assault on the North Pole?

2. If we doubled our group, how much farther could the expedition have gone?

3. If the pole were 60 miles away, how many people would have been needed? How about 70 miles? How about 100 miles?

4. How far could you go if you had 10 billion people?

A BEGINNING

Suppose we had just two people working together. We could successfully send one person 15 miles. Here is the diary of our expedition:

a) We left base camp together.

b) After 5 miles, I stored 5 miles worth of provisions, gave my friend 5 miles worth (replenishing her depleted store), and started back toward base camp.

117

c) I returned to camp, exhausting my provisions. My friend continued on for 10 more miles before turning around and coming back to our storage place 5 miles out.

d) Her provisions were exhausted when she reached the storage place, but the 5-miles worth of provisions that were stored there got her back safely to base camp.

42. The Fibonacci Factor

The most intriguing sequence in all mathematics is the Fibonacci sequence, named after Leonardo Fibonacci, an Italian who lived in the thirteenth century. The sequence begins with 1, 1, and then every succeeding term is found by adding the two preceding terms together. Thus it proceeds 1, 1, 2, 3, 5, 8, 13, 21, 34, 55, ... The sequence appears in several problems in the book, but this is the only problem devoted exclusively to it.

THE QUESTIONS

1. Where in the sequence will the smallest Fibonacci number occur that is divisible by all the primes less than 50?

2. What is the prime decomposition of the 120th Fibonacci number?

3. If written out, approximately how many digits will your answer to question 2 be? How about question 1?

4. Make a list of several divisibility properties that hold in the world of the Fibonacci numbers.

5. Analyze the sequence F_2/F_1, F_4/F_2, F_6/F_3, . . . (where F_n denotes the nth Fibonacci number).

A BEGINNING

Here is the prime decomposition of the first ten Fibonacci numbers:

Number of term	1	2	3	4	5	6	7	8	9	10
Fibonacci number	1	1	2	3	5	8	13	21	34	55
Prime decomposition			2	3	5	2^3	13	3×7	2×17	5×11

If you continue this list, you will find many surprising relationships. For example, you will find that every Fibonacci number that is divisible by 7 is also divisible by 3. This shows up first at the eighth term, which is 21.

Another observation you might make is that Fibonacci numbers that are prime tend to occur at the prime terms and vice versa. This is not entirely true because the prime Fibonacci number 3 is term number 4, a nonprime. But other than that, our table above shows that 2 is term number 3, 5 is term number 5, and 13 is term number 7.

43. Periodic Fractions

This problem continues the investigation of unit fractions, $1/n$, that was begun in chapter 2. In particular, the relationship between n and the period of the decimal expansion of $1/n$ is explored.

THE QUESTIONS

1. *a)* How many fractions k/n ($k < n$) have period 20?

   b) How many unit fractions, $1/n$, have period 20?

   c) For which primes p does $1/p$ have period 20?

2. Find the unit fraction with the smallest denominator that has period—

   a) 100;

   b) $2 \times 3 \times 5 \times 7 \times 11 \times 13$.

3. Suppose that $1/n$ and $1/m$ have the same period; call it t. What can you say about the period of $1/nm$? In particular:

   a) If $n \neq m$, under what circumstances does the period of $1/nm = t$?

   b) If $n = m$, when does the period of $1/nm = t$? In other words, when does the period of $1/n^2$ equal the period of $1/n$? (It obviously does when $n = 3$. Are there other examples?)

A BEGINNING

Let us look at proper fractions in decimal form with period 2. These fractions look like this:

$$0.\overline{ab}$$

Now a and b are whole numbers that take on any value from 0 to 9; so there are 100 values. But we must rule out $0.\overline{00}$ because it is 0; $0.\overline{99}$ because it is equal to 1; and $0.\overline{11}, 0.\overline{22}, \ldots, 0.\overline{88}$ because these decimals all have period 1. In fact, they are the fractions $1/9, 2/9, \ldots, 8/9$. This leaves us ninety fractions.

As for unit fractions, we found in chapter 2 that $1/11$ and $1/33$ have periods of 2. Are there any more? We can use a programmable calculator with the program suggested in chapter 2 and find out. All we need to do is search those fractions with denominators up to 99. We find that $1/99$ is the only other unit fraction with period 2. So, in all, there are three unit fractions that have period 2. The only one with a prime denominator is $1/11$.

44. The Universe of Fractions with a Prime Denominator

The word *universe* conjures up geometric images of centers and circles. The solar system is a universe with a sun at the center and planets moving around the sun in circular orbits. The planets, too, are the centers of their universes with moons circling around them. Then there is the infinitesimal universe of the atom with its electrons orbiting in their circular shells. We use this imagery here with the decimal expansions of proper fractions with a prime denominator. In chapter 2 we examined expansions of $1/n$ and found that if n did not have factors of 2 or 5, then $1/n$ had a repeating decimal expansion. For example, $1/7 = 0.\overline{142857}$. But notice that the other proper fractions with 7 in the denominator have the same six numbers appearing in the same circular order:

$$2/7 = 0.\overline{285714}$$
$$3/7 = 0.\overline{428571}$$
$$4/7 = 0.\overline{571428}$$
$$5/7 = 0.\overline{714285}$$
$$6/7 = 0.\overline{857142}$$

We shall write these numbers in a circle in figure 8.1. Notice that if a decimal point is placed between two of the numbers, a periodic expansion is formed. It is the decimal representation of one of the six proper fractions with denominator 7. For example, if the point is placed between the 1 and the 4 and you move clockwise once around the circle, you get .428 571. Continuing your trip around the ring (and removing the decimal point), you will spin out .428 571 428 571 428 . . . , the expansion of 3/7. We shall call this circle a *ring* of the number 7. The number of numerals in the circle will be referred to as the *size* of the ring.

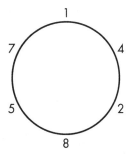

Fig. 8.1

Although 7 has just one ring, there are examples of primes with more than one ring. Below is a listing of the decimal expansions of the proper fractions with 13 as the denominator.

1/13 = 0.076923 . . .	7/13 = 0.538461 . . .
2/13 = 0.153846 . . .	8/13 = 0.615384 . . .
3/13 = 0.230769 . . .	9/13 = 0.692307 . . .
4/13 = 0.307692 . . .	10/13 = 0.769230 . . .
5/13 = 0.384615 . . .	11/13 = 0.846153 . . .
6/13 = 0.461538 . . .	12/13 = 0.923076 . . .

These twelve expansions form two distinct cyclic sequences of numbers. So 13 has two rings, both of size 6 (see fig. 8.2).

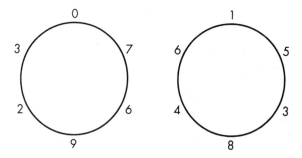

Fig. 8.2

THE QUESTIONS

1. Consider all the primes less than 1000:

   a) Which prime has the biggest ring? How big is it?

   b) Which prime has the most rings? How many does it have?

   c) How many primes have only one ring?

   d) How many have only two rings?

2. Find the smallest prime that has—

   a) a ring larger than 1000;

   b) more than 1000 rings.

Universes are mysterious places. Some phenomena are explainable; some are not. Examine these questions and try to figure out which can be answered with a logical explanation and which remain mysterious.

3. *a)* Are all rings of a single prime the same size?

   b) Suppose that the sizes of the rings of a prime are even. What can you say about the numbers that are diametrically opposite each other in the ring?

c) If the size of the rings is divisible by 3, what can you say about the numbers that are 120° apart?

d) If you move your decimal point around the ring through a fixed number of numbers (from one expansion to another), what can you say about the relationship between the two fractions (represented by the two expansions)? If a prime has more than one ring, does your answer vary with each ring?

e) In a prime with several rings, how can you tell if two fractions belong to the same ring?

4. *a*) Suppose your prime has a single ring. If the prime ends in a 1, what can you say about the frequency that each digit occurs in the ring? If your prime ends in a 3, can you say anything? How about primes ending in a 7? In a 9?

b) Address questions (*a*) for primes that have more than one ring. Can you say anything about the frequencies of digits occurring in each ring? In all rings taken together?

5. There is a theory that the universe was originally made up of 9s. Later these 9s split up into the numbers that form the rings of primes that we know today. Try to give validity to this theory in as many different ways as you can.

This universe is infinitely large, and naturally, there are things that cannot be known for certain. There are, however, tendencies that seem to be true. Try to give validity, or at least credibility, to these statements. You may want to change or sharpen them.

6. *a*) There are twice as many prime numbers with even-sized rings as with odd-sized rings.

b) For each number *n*, there is a prime that has rings of size *n*.

c) Three out of eight primes have one ring.

d) Two out of seven primes have two rings.

e) As many primes have an even number of rings as have an odd number of rings.

f) For each number *n*, there is a prime with that number of rings.

A BEGINNING

Chapter 2 gives us a good beginning for this investigation. Using the programs suggested there, we can find the data in table 8.1.

Analyzing the data, we find that 97 has the largest ring, size 96, and 37

has the most rings, 12. Also, nine of the twenty-three primes have just one
ring—that makes 39 percent, and eight have two rings—that makes 35
percent. Thirteen primes have rings of even size; ten have odd size. Twelve
primes have an even number of rings; eleven have an odd number.

Table 8.1
Rings of the Twenty-three Primes Less than 100 (Excluding 2 and 5)

Prime	Ring size	Number of rings		Prime	Ring size	Number of rings
3	1	2		47	46	1
7	6	1		53	13	4
11	2	5		59	58	1
13	6	2		61	60	1
17	16	1		67	33	2
19	18	1		71	35	2
23	22	1		73	8	9
29	28	1		79	13	6
31	15	2		83	41	2
37	3	12		89	44	2
41	5	8		97	96	1
43	21	2				

45. Aw, Cm'on, Coach, I'll Be Here All Day

I am a terrific basketball player except for one thing—I can't shoot free throws. My basketball coach is fed up. He tells me that until I improve, I have to stay after practice every day and shoot free throws. I can't go home until I have made several consecutive free throws. He hasn't yet told me what "several" means. Suppose it means just one (fat chance!). With some figuring, I should be able to tell how many shots it should take to make one in a row.

Since I am a 50 percent free-throw shooter, half the time I should accomplish this goal in one shot. Not bad. And if I miss, I can try again. Only 25 percent of the time would I expect to miss both shots. That means 75 percent of the time I will achieve my goal in two shots.

Looking at it another way, if I stayed after practice for sixteen days and shot free throws, I could expect that half of the time, or eight of those times, I would make the first shot. One-quarter of the time, or four times, it would take two shots (the chances that I miss the first shot and make the second are $(1/2)(1/2) = 1/4$). Continuing like this: one-eighth of the time, or twice, it would take three shots; one-sixteenth of the time, or once, it would take four shots. The other time it would take five or more shots.

So the average number of shots needed to complete the task would be

$$\frac{1+1+1+1+1+1+1+1+2+2+2+2+3+3+4+5^+}{16} = \frac{31^+}{16}.$$

This is almost 2. So, on average, I would expect to complete the task in about two shots.

THE QUESTIONS

Suppose that you are a 50 percent free-throw shooter.

1. Your coach asks that you keep shooting until you make two in a row.

   a) On average, how many times would you expect to have to shoot to make two in a row?

   b) How many times will you be shooting if you expect to have approximately a 50 percent chance of doing this? A 75 percent chance? A 90 percent chance?

2. Answer the same questions as in 1(*a*) and 1(*b*) if your coach asks you to keep shooting until you make—

   a) three in a row;

b) four in a row;

c) five in a row.

3. Your coach insists that you keep shooting until you make ten in a row.

a) On average, how many shots will it take?

b) How many shots would you expect to shoot to have approximately a 50 percent chance of doing this?

4. Suppose that all this practice has paid off.

a) If you are a 75 percent shooter, on average, how many shots will it take to make ten in a row?

b) If you are a 90 percent shooter, how many shots will it take to make ten in a row?

5. If you figure that 125 free throws will, on average, meet your coach's demands, how long a string of consecutive baskets did he insist on if you are a—

a) 50 percent shooter?

b) 75 percent shooter?

c) 90 percent shooter?

A BEGINNING

Let us look at the situation for a 50 percent free-throw shooter trying to make two shots in a row. We shall use the notation S for success and F for failure. Some scenarios appear in figure 8.3.

Scenario	Number of shots	Chances for success
S S	2	1/4
F S S	3	1/8
S F S S	4	1/16
F F S S		1/16
S F F S S	5	1/32
F S F S S		1/32
F F F S S		1/32

Fig. 8.3

Notice that if we take at least four shots, we can expect to make two of them in succession at least $1/4 + 1/8 + 1/16 + 1/16 = 1/2$ of the time. We have answered one part of our first question! It takes four shots to have a 50 percent chance of meeting our goal. And with five shots we can expect to meet our goal $1/4 + 1/8 + 1/8 + 3/32 = 59.4$ percent of the time.

If we perform this experiment thirty-two times, we can expect that eight times we will be successful with two shots, four times with three shots, four times with four shots, three times with five shots, and thirteen times will take six or more shots. It looks as if we should look at more scenarios; if we are unable to pin down an answer thirteen times out of thirty-two, we don't know enough to answer the question about the average number of tries.

46. I'll Take the Lamborghini

The king is looking for a rich wife, and he is willing to give a car to the lucky person who can pick her out. There are 1000 eligible women, and each has written her net worth on a postcard and dropped it in a drum. As it turns out, every dollar amount is different. Every ten seconds for the next two hours, forty-six minutes, and forty seconds, the king will draw a card from the drum and announce its dollar value. Greedy, smart car lovers like me have taken on the challenge of picking out the richest woman. Here is our problem. After a dollar amount is read, we will have just ten seconds to make up our minds about that particular woman and lock in our choice. If we let the time elapse, then that woman can no longer be our choice. If two or more people correctly pick the richest woman, the person who locked in the choice first will win the car.

I have adopted the following strategy. I will record the first several dollar values to get a feeling for how rich these women are. After an appropriate recording period I will choose the first woman whose worth exceeds the highest value that I have recorded up to that point.

If the richest woman has already passed by while I was busy recording net worths, then I am stuck with choosing the final woman, whatever her worth.

THE QUESTIONS

1. For best results, how many women should I let pass by before I get serious about choosing one?

2. With this strategy, what are my best chances of actually picking the richest woman and owning that car?

A BEGINNING

Let us assume that there are only four women, and let us label their net worths from largest to smallest a, b, c, and d. There are twenty-four ways that these values can be announced, as shown in the chart in figure 8.4.

1	2	3	4
a, b, c, d	b, a, c, d	b, c, a, d	b, c, d, a
a, b, d, c	b, a, d, c	b, d, a, c	b, d, c, a
a, c, b, d	c, a, b, d	c, b, a, d	c, b, d, a
a, c, d, b	c, a, d, b	c, d, a, b	c, d, b, a
a, d, b, c	d, a, b, c	d, b, a, c	d, b, c, a
a, d, c, b	d, a, c, b	d, c, a, b	d, c, b, a

Fig. 8.4

Our strategy gives us the following possibilities:

1. If we choose the very first woman, that will be successful in all six instances listed in column 1. That choice won't work in any other column, however. Thus, if we have no recording period at all, our chances of picking the richest woman is 1/4.

2. If we choose to let one woman go by, record her worth, and then choose (if she exists) the first woman that is richer, our chances for success are greater. All possibilities listed in column 2 are successful, furthermore, three from 3 (*b, c, a, d; b, d, a, c;* and *c, d, a, b*) and two from 4 (*b, c, d, a;* and *b, d, c, a*) are successful. This makes a total of 11. The probability of picking the richest woman is then

$$(1/4) \ (6/6 \ + \ 3/6 \ + \ 2/6) \ = \ 11/24.$$

3. If we let two women go by before actively searching, we should count the successes from column 3 [6] and column 4 [4]. The probability for success is

$$1/4 \ (6/6 \ + \ 4/6) \ = \ 10/24.$$

4. If we let three women go by, the probability is clearly 1/4.

The chart below summarizes the results:

Number of women observed	Probability of success
0	1/4
1	11/24
2	10/24
3	1/4

So for this simplification, we find that the best strategy is to let one woman pass by. This will allow the probability for success in choosing the richest to be the best possible: 11/24, or about .458.

47. The Number 1 Is Truly #1

The question here is easy to state: Pick a number, any number. What are the chances that the number picked begins with a 1?

The trouble with this question is that it is difficult to deal with the concept of "any number." There are an infinite number of positive integers. How shall we make a finite list of the integers so that we can tally those that begin with a 1? Mathematicians refer to *any numbers* as *random numbers,* and the problem of generating lists of random numbers is not at all easy. Here we shall try two ways. In one way, we will let Mother Nature do it; that is, we will use natural phenomena that can be measured, such as heights of mountains, lengths of rivers, and atomic weights of elements, and collect a list of numbers from these. In the second way, we will use technology—the computer. Computers have random-number generators that try to do what we are asking here.

THE QUESTIONS

1. Make a list of 500 random numbers from lists of measurements in an almanac.

   a) What percentage of the numbers begins with a 1?

   b) What percentage begins with a 2? A 3, . . ., a 9?

   c) What happens to your list if you change the units of measure? For example, you might change feet to inches, or square miles to square feet.

2. *a)* Using your random-number generator, create a list of 500 numbers between 1 and 10 million (you may call them $a_1, a_2, \ldots, a_{500}$). Answer questions 1 (*a*) and 1 (*b*) for your list. Are the answers what you would expect?

   b) Using you list of 500 numbers from 2 (*a*), generate a second list of 500 numbers where each new number, b_1, is a random number between 1 and a_1. Again answer questions 1 (*a*) and 1 (*b*) for this list. What is happening?

   c) Continue in this fashion with lists c_1 (random numbers between 1 and b_1) and d_1 (random numbers between 1 and c_1) until the percentages found for the initial occurrences of the numbers 1, 2, . . ., 9 become relatively stable. How do these percentages compare to those of question 1?

3. Take your list from 1 and your list from 2 (*c*):

   a) Double every number. How does that affect the distribution of first digits?

   b) Multiply every number by pi. How does this affect the distribution? (Multiplying by pi generates numbers that are not integers, but still you can pick out the initial digit.)

    c) Operate on your list in other mathematical ways and see how the distribution is affected.

    4. Consider the first several terms of different sequences of whole numbers. Examine how the length of the sequence affects the distribution of first digits.

    5. Formulate a theory about the distribution of first digits of certain sets of numbers. Include in your theory not only a description of the certain sets but also the mathematical operations that can transform one set into another set without significantly altering this distribution.

A BEGINNING

    When drawing up a list of 500 numbers from an almanac, you can use, along with natural phenomena, population charts for cities or countries and measurements of constructed phenomena such as areas of countries, states, and national parks.

    For the random-number generator, recall from chapter 5 that you can produce a list of random numbers between 1 and 10 million with the following program:

```
10 N = 1
20 A = INT(RND(1)*10000000 + 1)
30 PRINT A
40 N = N+1
50 IF N > 500 GOTO 70
60 GOTO 20
70 END
```

Since the number 10 million is always the upper bound on the set of numbers randomly picked, the resulting list (which we have labeled a_1, a_2, . . . in question 2 (a)) is probably not very random in its distribution of first digits. However, if the upper bounds on the sets are themselves somewhat random, then the computer's random choice within these sets has a better chance of being truly random. You can generate a second list with flexible upper bounds from the first list by making one addition and one alteration to the program above:

```
25 B = INT(RND(1)*A + 1)
30 PRINT B
```

This second list (which we have labeled b_1, b_2, . . . in question 2 (b)), although perhaps not yet random in its distribution, can then be used as upper bounds for the sets in a third series of computer-generated random numbers.

There are many sequences that occur in mathematics. Of course, the most basic is the sequence of natural numbers: 1, 2, 3, ... Also, there are the sequence of squares: 1, 4, 9, . . .; the sequence of powers of 2: 2, 4, 8, . . .; and the famous Fibonacci sequence: 1, 1, 2, 3, 5, ... Nor do we need to stay with whole-number sequences. We can check out the reciprocals of the natural numbers: 1, 1/2, 1/3, . . .; the square roots of natural number: $\sqrt{1}$, $\sqrt{2}$, $\sqrt{3}$, . . .; and the powers of zany numbers like pi.

Looking at the sequence of whole numbers, we find that two (1 and 10) of the first ten numbers begin with a 1. That makes 20 percent. However, in the first twenty numbers there are eleven numbers that begin with 1. That is 55 percent—a dramatic change. The powers-of-2 sequence contains three (16, 128, and 1024) in the first ten that begin with a 1 and six in the first twenty that begin with a 1. That is 30 percent for both. Naturally, many more terms in a sequence must be checked before we can make a judgment about the stability of the distribution of first digits.

48. Pythagorean Stars in the Night Sky

The night sky is filled with stars, but only a few of them are of any interest to us. Those are the very special stars that are located at an integral distance from our telescope. Our telescope is positioned at the origin. We will perform our analysis here with the stars in the first octant. All stars are located at points (x, y, z) where x, y, and z are integers. In the first octant, the coordinates x, y, and z are positive integers. The stars are called Pythagorean because $x^2 + y^2 + z^2 = d^2$ where d is also an integer.

THE QUESTIONS

1. If our telescope has a range of 100 units, how many stars can it see?

2. How does the population of visible stars increase if the range of the telescope doubles?

3. What is the approximate range of the telescope if 1 million stars are visible?

4. What is the approximate range of the telescope if 1 million constellations are visible?

5. Of all the constellations in question 4, which one appears smallest, that is, has its stars most closely bunched?

A BEGINNING

The closest stars are located at $(1, 2, 2)$, $(2, 1, 2)$, and $(2, 2, 1)$. The distance from our telescope to any of these stars is 3 (because $2^2 + 2^2 + 1^2 = 3^2$). These three stars form a constellation. A constellation comprises all stars that have the same coordinates in any order. Most constellations have six stars. If your telescope has a range of at least 7, it can pick up the constellation

$$(2, 3, 6), (2, 6, 3), (3, 2, 6), (3, 6, 2), (6, 2, 3), (6, 3, 2).$$

To find these special stars, you can use a computer program, or you can use a technique analogous to that used in the problem "A Population Explosion on the Rational Circle" in chapter 7.

49. A Plethora of Patterns in Continued Fraction Expansions

A continued fraction is a number of the form shown in figure 8.5.

$$a_0 + \cfrac{1}{a_1 + \cfrac{1}{a_2 + \cfrac{1}{a_3 + \cfrac{1}{a_4 + \cfrac{1}{a_5 + \cfrac{1}{\cdots}}}}}}$$

Fig. 8.5

We shall use shorthand and denote this form by

$$[a_0; a_1, a_2, \ldots, a_m, \ldots].$$

If the continued fraction has a repeating pattern, we denote it this way:

$$[a_0; \overline{a_1, \ldots, a_n}]$$

We say that the period of this continued fraction is n.

If the continued fraction has a finite expansion, then it is just a regular fraction. For example, $[1; 2, 2]$ is the number

$$1 + \cfrac{1}{2 + \cfrac{1}{2}},$$

which equals 7/5.

If the continued fraction is infinite and has a repetitive pattern, then it is known that the number represented is an irrational root of a quadratic equation with integral coefficients. The converse of this is also true. The questions below concern only roots of those quadratic equations of the form $x^2 - n = 0$ where n is not a perfect square. In other words, here we will look only at those continued fractions that represent square roots of numbers that are not perfect squares.

Continued fractions have fascinated mathematicians for centuries, and a lot is known about them. Surprisingly, there is a lot that is not known, however, and it remains a fascination to amateurs and professionals alike. The aspect that makes these expansions so attractive to us is the wealth of number patterns that arise. Some are obvious. For example, if the number $[n; \overline{a_1, \ldots, a_k}]$ represents an irrational square root, then $a_k = 2n$. (Of course, even the obvious should be explained; so there is always the challenge of proving a theorem.) Some of the patterns are incredibly obscure. In any case, if you are a pattern seeker, this is the ideal problem for you.

THE QUESTIONS

1. How can you tell which of these two numbers is larger?

$$N = [n; \overline{a_1, \ldots, a_j}]$$
$$M = [m; \overline{b_1, \ldots, b_k}]$$

2. For a given integer n, how many continued fractions of the form $[n; \overline{a_1, \ldots, 2a}]$—

   a) begin their period with a 1 (i.e., $a_1 = 1$)?

   b) begin their period with a 2? With a 3? With an n?

Let us consider those numbers of the form $[n; \overline{a_1, \ldots, 2N}]$ where $n \leq 1000$. In other words, let us look at those numbers $\sqrt{N}$ where $N \leq 1\,000\,000$ and N is not a perfect square.

3. Which n has the most expansions of period 2? How many does it have?

4. Which n has the most expansions of period 4 with the period beginning 1? How many does it have?

5. Which n has the most expansions of period 6 with the period beginning 1, 1? How many does it have?

6. a) For what number N does $\sqrt{N}$ have the most successive 1's in its expansion?

   b) For what N would $\sqrt{N}$ have 100 successive 1's in its expansion?

7. a) Estimate the size of the largest period of $\sqrt{N}$ (for $N \leq 1\,000\,000$).

   b) Find the smallest N such that $\sqrt{N}$ has a period of at least 1000.

8. Comment on the following statements:

   a) If m appears in the expansion of $[n; \overline{a_1, \ldots, 2n}]$, then $m < n$.

   b) If n appears in the expansion of $[n; \overline{a_1, \ldots, 2n}]$, then it appears only once and in the middle.

   c) If $n - 1$ appears in the expansion of $[n; \overline{a_1, \ldots, 2n}]$, then it appears only once and in the middle.

   d) There is no n whose expansion $[n; \overline{a_1, \ldots, 2n}]$ is all 1's (except for the final term) that has period $3k$.

   e) There are periods of any size.

   f) There are periods that begin with any sequence $a_1, a_2, \ldots, a_k$.

A BEGINNING

First, we must write a program that will print out the continued fraction expansions. Figure 8.6 shows the continued fraction expansions for $\sqrt{N}$ where $N \leq 25$. Thus $n \leq 4$ in these expansions.

$\sqrt{2} = [1; \overline{2}]$ $\sqrt{11} = [3; \overline{3, 6}]$ $\sqrt{19} = [4; \overline{4, 8}]$

$\sqrt{3} = [1; \overline{1, 2}]$ $\sqrt{12} = [3; \overline{2, 6}]$ $\sqrt{20} = [4; \overline{2, 8}]$

$\sqrt{5} = [2; \overline{4}]$ $\sqrt{13} = [3; \overline{1, 1, 1, 1, 6}]$ $\sqrt{21} = [4; \overline{1, 1, 2, 1, 1, 8}]$

$\sqrt{6} = [2; \overline{2, 4}]$ $\sqrt{14} = [3; \overline{1, 2, 1, 6}]$ $\sqrt{22} = [4; \overline{1, 2, 4, 2, 1, 8}]$

$\sqrt{7} = [2; \overline{1, 1, 1, 4}]$ $\sqrt{15} = [3; \overline{1, 6}]$ $\sqrt{23} = [4; \overline{1, 3, 1, 8}]$

$\sqrt{8} = [2; \overline{1, 4}]$ $\sqrt{17} = [4; \overline{8}]$ $\sqrt{24} = [4; \overline{1, 8}]$

$\sqrt{10} = [3; \overline{6}]$ $\sqrt{18} = [4; \overline{4, 8}]$

Fig. 8.6

As mentioned above, it appears that the last term of $[n; \overline{a_1, \ldots, a_k}]$ is always twice n; that is, $a_k = 2n$. Also, it seems that the expansions are symmetric about a middle. This is, if the expansion is $[n; \overline{a_1, \ldots, a_j, 2n}]$, then $a_1 = a_j$; $a_2 = a_{j-1}$; and so on.

In our small sample, we may notice the following facts that bear on our questions: For $n = 3$, there are three expansions of period 2. That is the most such expansions for any $n \leq 4$. There is one example of an expansion of period 4 beginning with a 1. It is for $\sqrt{14} = [3; \overline{1, 2, 1, 6}]$. There is also one example of an expansion of period 6 beginning with 1, 1. It is $\sqrt{21} = [4; \overline{1, 1, 2, 1, 1, 8}]$. The longest sequence of consecutive 1's is four, and it belongs to the number $\sqrt{13}$—$\sqrt{13} = [3; \overline{1, 1, 1, 1, 6}]$.

50. A Bridge of Cards with a Harmonic Span

Notice that if you place three cards at the end of a table as in figure 8.7, they will not fall over. Place the first card flush with the end of the table, the second card on top of the first with 1/3 of it hanging over the edge, and the third card on top of the second with 1/2 of it extending beyond the second card. This threesome of cards will not fall off the table; *at least they won't if the cards are sticky enough to cling together.* The diagram in figure 8.7 illustrates this configuration of cards.

(*Note*: The dots (●) represent the centers of gravity.)

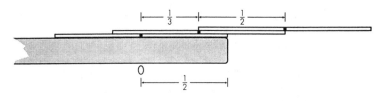

Fig. 8.7

The cards stay on the table because the center of gravity of the group lies above the table. The center of gravity of this unit is the average of the centers of gravity of the individual cards. We shall assume that the length of a card is 1, and, as shown in the figure, we will position 0 at the bottom card's center of gravity. Then the cards immediately above are centered at 1/3 and (1/3 + 1/2) = 5/6. The average of 0, 1/3, and 5/6 is (7/6)/3, which is 7/18. This is less than 1/2, which is the edge of the table in our measuring scheme. The top card in this example extends 1/2 + 1/3 = 5/6 over the edge of the table. So if we have two tables and six cards, we can have a bridge of cards whose span is 5/6 + 5/6 = 5/3.

Generally speaking, a harmonic span consists of cards extending $1/n$, $1/(n + 1)$, $1/(n + 2)$, . . . , units beyond their immediate support cards. Building on our span in the figure, we can move the base card over 1/4 to the right, leave the upper two cards in their relative positions, and slip in a fourth card at the bottom as our new base card. Now the cards extend 1/2, 1/3, and 1/4, respectively, over their immediate support card. The average of the centers of gravity of these four cards is

$$1/4 \,(0 + 1/4 + (1/4 + 1/3) + (1/4 + 1/3 + 1/2)) = 23/48.$$

Since 23/48 < 1/2, this set of cards will not fall over.

Now the top card extends 1/4 + 1/3 + 1/2 = 13/12 beyond the edge of the table; so it is entirely to the right of the table—it is in midair! If we put a symmetric group on the right, we will have a bridge that spans 13/6 (or about 2.167) units.

If we continue to slip in new base cards, we run into problems. If we move this group 1/5 to the right and tuck in a fifth card as our new base card, the group will topple. Here's why. The centers of gravity of these five cards are, respectively,

0;

1/5;

(1/5 + 1/4);

(1/5 + 1/4 + 1/3);

(1/5 + 1/4 + 1/3 + 1/2).

The average of these is

$$1/5 \ (4/5 \ + \ 3/4 \ + \ 2/3 \ + \ 1/2) \ = \ 163/300,$$

which is > 1/2. Because the center of gravity of this group of five cards lies 3/300 of a unit beyond the edge of the table, the group falls over.

But we don't need to give up. We have two options. We can remove the top card, which extends 1/2 unit beyond its neighbor below, and slip in a card at the bottom. Specifically, if we put down a new base card and move the remaining group 1/6 to the right of this, we can check and see that the group will stand. In fact, we can slip another card in and move the group 1/7 to the right and find that the group will stand.

Our other option would be to add a second base card flush with the edge of the table. This extra base card changes the center of gravity and, in this instance, solves the problem. The six-card unit will now stand.

THE QUESTIONS

Suppose that you have two decks of cards, 52 cards in each deck.

1. *a*) Using all cards, what is the maximum harmonic span you can create using a single base card flush with the table?

b) Can you get a wider span by using fewer than 52 cards in each deck? If so, how many should you use for the maximum span?

c) In question (*b*), how many cards are entirely in midair?

2. *a*) What is the maximum harmonic span you can create using multiple base cards flush with the table?

b) Can you get an equally wide span with fewer than 52 cards in each deck? If so, how many would you use?

c) In (*b*), how many are base cards and how many are span cards?

Suppose you allow the use of up to 1000 cards in each deck.

3. *a*) What is the maximum span you can create using a single base card? What percentage of the cards is in midair?

   b) What is the maximum span you can create using multiple base cards? What is the ratio of base cards to span cards?

4. If you had a trillion cards in each deck, estimate—

   a) the maximum span you could get using a single base card and the percentage of the cards that would be in midair;

   b) the maximum span you could get using multiple base cards and the percentage of the cards that would be base cards.

5. The questions above were based on a harmonic span named after the famous harmonic series $1 + 1/2 + 1/3 + \ldots + 1/n + \ldots$. Suppose you build your bridges with harmonic-like spans based on such harmonic-like series as $1/2 + 1/4 + \ldots + 1/2n + \ldots$ or $1/3 + 1/6 + \ldots + 1/3n + \ldots$. Can you get wider spans?

A BEGINNING

We have already made some headway in our introduction. We can check the statements above about our new six-card groups.

For the six cards built on a single base card, the centers of gravity extend beyond their support by 0, 1/7, 1/6, 1/5, 1/4, and 1/3, respectively. The respective centers of gravity of the individual cards are

0;

1/7;

(1/7 + 1/6);

(1/7 + 1/6 + 1/5);

(1/7 + . . . + 1/4);

(1/7 + . . . + 1/3).

The center of gravity of the group is

$$1/6 \ (6/7 + 5/6 + 4/5 + 3/4 + 2/3) = 1182/2520,$$

which is < 1/2. So the center of gravity lies 78/2520 (about 0.031) from the edge of the table.

Here the top card extends $1/7 + 1/6 + 1/5 + 1/4 + 1/3 = 459/420$ (about 1.093) beyond the edge of the table. Putting an equivalent set of cards on another table, we can create a span of distance 459/210, or about 2.186. This is better than the 2.167 we created with eight cards.

In this example the number of cards in midair is four. The two top cards on each side are entirely off the edges of their tables.

For the six cards built on a multiple base of two cards, their centers of gravity extend beyond their support by 0, 0, 1/5, 1/4, 1/3, and 1/2. The centers of gravity of the individual cards are

0;

0;

1/5;

(1/5 + 1/4);

(1/5 + 1/4 + 1/3);

(1/5 + 1/4 + 1/3 + 1/2).

The center of gravity of the group is

$$1/6 \ (4/5 + 3/4 + 2/3 + 1/2) = 163/360 < 1/2.$$

In this arrangement, the top card extends $1/5 + 1/4 + 1/3 + 1/2 = 1.283$ beyond the edge of the table; so by putting an equivalent set of cards on an opposite table, we can create a record span of 2.567. We accomplished this with two base cards and four span cards.

51. A Snow Job

Early this morning it started to snow. Before long, the snow plow began clearing the road, and when I got up two hours later, the road was clear for fifteen miles. The plow had cleared ten miles during the first hour and five miles during the second hour. The snow is still falling at a constant rate, and the plow is presumably removing it at a constant rate, too. Because of this, I figure that the rate at which the plow is moving forward is inversely proportional to the passage of time. After all, the amount of snow that the plow must face at any moment is directly proportional to the time that has passed since the snow began; so, obviously, the job becomes harder and harder as time passes. What I don't know is when the snow started to fall.

THE QUESTIONS

1. How long before the plow began did the snow start falling—

   a) to the nearest minute?

   b) to the nearest second?

2. How far will the plow progress during—

   a) the third hour?

   b) the fourth hour?

3. How long will it take the plow to clear another fifteen miles?

A BEGINNING

Let us first address these questions by finding answers that are correct to the nearest half hour. Our procedure will be to guess an answer and then check to see how good the guess is. Our first guess will be that the plow begins at the same time the snow begins.

We will adopt the following notation:

s_1 is the distance in miles that the plow travels during the first half hour

s_2 is the distance traveled during the second half hour

s_3 is the distance traveled during the third half hour

s_4 is the distance traveled during the fourth half hour

Letting $v(t)$ stand for the velocity at time t, we have the equation $v(t) = k/t$ where k is a constant of proportionality. This equation expresses our assumption that the velocity of the plow is inversely proportional to the time elapsed.

In order to find s_1, we will guess at an average velocity of the plow over the first half hour and multiply it by the time elapsed (one-half hour). The velocity at the midpoint, fifteen minutes, seems reasonable. Thus $s_1 = (v(1/4))(1/2) = (k/(1/4))(1/2)$. Making similar assumptions for the other distances, we come up with the following approximations for s_1, s_2, s_3, and s_4, the respective distances traveled over the first two hours.

$$s_1 = \frac{k}{1/4} (1/2)$$

$$s_2 = \frac{k}{3/4} (1/2)$$

$$s_3 = \frac{k}{5/4} (1/2)$$

$$s_4 = \frac{k}{7/4} (1/2)$$

Notice that we choose the times $t = 3/4, 5/4$, and $7/4$ because those are the halfway points within the half-hour intervals—$[1/2, 1]$, $[1, 3/2]$, $[3/2, 2]$, respectively. Since the plow travels twice as far during the first hour as during the second, we can write this equation:

$$s_1 + s_2 = 2(s_3 + s_3)$$

Using algebra, we get

$$k(2 + 2/3) = 2k(2/5 + 2/7).$$

This leads to $(8/3)k = (48/35)k$, which is not a correct equation. This tells us something that we suspected; the snow and the plow did not start at the same time. But we can learn something more from this calculation. The ratio of $(8/3)k$ to $(48/35)k$ can be used as a numerical evaluation of how accurate our guess is. If this ratio is close to 1, then our guess is close to reality. We will call this ratio the *accuracy index*. More precisely, the accuracy index is the fraction formed by the two numbers d_1 and $2d_2$ where d_1 and d_2 represent the distances traveled in the first mile and the second mile. For convenience we will take the larger of these two values to be the numerator of the fraction, so that the accuracy index will always be greater than 1. Now in this example, the accuracy index is $(8/3)k/(48/35)k = 1.94$. We won't know how good an index this is until we try other scenarios.

Let us now suppose that one-half hour elapses before the plow starts nd do the calculations again. Then we have

$$s_1 = \frac{k}{(3/4)} (1/2)$$

$$s_2 = \frac{k}{(5/4)} (1/2)$$

$$s_3 = \frac{k}{(7/4)} \, (1/2)$$

$$s_4 = \frac{k}{(9/4)} \, (1/2).$$

We find that

$$s_1 + s_2 = 2k(1/3 + 1/5)$$
$$2(s_3 + s_4) = 4k(1/7 + 1/9).$$

The accuracy index here is 1.05. This number is much closer to 1 than 1.94 is; so this guess is more accurate. We can try other scenarios; for example, the plow leaves one hour after the snow begins, but we will find that the most accurate guess is the one just made—the plow leaves one-half hour after the snow begins.

Using this answer we can find out approximately how far the plow went in the third hour. We know that $s_1 + s_2 = 10$ (exactly), and $s_1 + s_2 = 2k(1/3 + 1/5)$ (approximately); so $k = 9.375$.

Similarly, knowing two pieces of information about $s_3 + s_4$, we get

$$s_3 + s_4 = 2k(1/7 + 1/9) = 5;$$

so $k = 9.844$. Because we are only approximating k, we will choose the average of these two, 9.61, and proceed. The distance traveled during the third hour will be represented by $s_5 + s_6$ where $s_5 = v(11/4) \, (1/2)$ and $s_6 = v(13/4) \, (1/2)$. So we get

$$s_5 = 2k(1/11)$$
$$s_6 = 2k(1/13).$$

Letting $k = 9.61$, we get for the third hour 3.226 miles. We will get a better fix on this distance when we get a finer approximation of the time the snow began to fall.

Continuing this approximation procedure, we find that our next step will be to consider the best possible answer to the nearest one-third of an hour. Again we will split up that two-hour interval, this time into six time segments of twenty minutes apiece. We will alter our notation so that $s_1, s_2, s_3, \ldots$ are distances traveled in successive twenty-minute periods. Again we will average the rates of progress of the plow at times halfway within the intervals. That would be at times $t = 1/6, 3/6, 5/6, \ldots$. If we assume that the plow starts one-third of an hour after the snow begins, we get the following equations:

$$s_1 + s_2 + s_3 = 2k(1/3 + 1/5 + 1/7)$$
$$2(s_4 + s_5 + s_6) = 4k(1/9 + 1/11 + 1/13)$$

144

EXPLORATORY PROBLEMS IN MATHEMATICS

The ratio of the larger value to the smaller is 1.212. This guess is not as accurate as the earlier one, so we will abandon it and try the next guess— the plow starts two-thirds of an hour after the snow starts falling. Table 8.2 records our results.

Table 8.2
Accuracy of Our Guesses

Time elapse before the plow begins (in hours)	Interval of accuracy (in hours)	Accuracy index
0	1/2	1.94
1/2	1/2	1.05
1/3	1/3	1.212
2/3	1/3	?

We have underlined in the table the best approximation so far. We should continue this procedure, making a list of only the best new approximations.

52. Are the Natural Numbers Overweight?

Natural numbers, like the rest of us, are weight conscious. Some are too fat, some are too thin, and some are just right. The weight of a number is related to its multiplicative makeup; in particular, it is the ratio of the sum of its factors to itself. A number is *perfect* if the sum of its factors equals twice the number itself. If the sum falls short of twice the number, the number is said to be *underweight*; if it exceeds twice the number, it is said to be *overweight*. In mathematical literature, the respective terms are *deficient* and *abundant* (*perfect* is used in the literature). A number is a *hunk* if the sum of its factors is exactly three times, or four times, or any integral number (greater than 2) of times larger than itself.

THE QUESTIONS

A weight census of the first 1 million natural numbers (excluding 1) is taken.

1. Which number is the most underweight? Which is the most overweight?

2. List all the perfect numbers that you can find.

3. What percentage of the numbers is overweight? What percentage of evens is overweight? What percentage of odds is overweight?

4. What is the average obesity quotient of the population? Of the even numbers? Of the odd numbers?

5. From this census, formulate a theory on what makes numbers heavy. In your theory, find a relationship between the obesity quotients of n and kn where n is a natural number and kn is a multiple of n.

6. Find the smallest number with obesity quotient > 10. If your answer is an even number, then if possible, find the smallest odd number with obesity quotient > 10.

7. Find as many hunks as you can. What is the heaviest hunk you can find?

A BEGINNING

The obesity quotient is used to measure the weight of a number. This quotient, Q, is defined as the sum of the factors divided by the number. Let us look at the population of the numbers from 2 through 10:

$$Q(2) = (1 + 2)/2 = 3/2$$
$$Q(3) = (1 + 3)/3 = 4/3$$
$$Q(4) = (1 + 2 + 4)/4 = 7/4$$
$$Q(5) = (1 + 5)/5 = 6/5$$
$$Q(6) = (1 + 2 + 3 + 6)/6 = 12/6 = 2$$
$$Q(7) = (1 + 7)/7 = 8/7$$
$$Q(8) = (1 + 2 + 4 + 8)/8 = 15/8$$
$$Q(9) = (1 + 3 + 9)/9 = 13/9$$
$$Q(10) = (1 + 2 + 5 + 10)/10 = 9/5$$

The most underweight number is 7; the heaviest is the perfect number 6. All the numbers, with the exception of 6, are underweight. The average obesity quotient of the population is 1.56. The even numbers average to 1.785, and the average of the odd numbers is 1.28.

53. Making Triangles out of Straws

This is a twist on the game of drawing straws to see who wins. Instead of having each person draw one straw, with the longer straws beating the shorter ones, we have each person draw three straws. If your straws cannot form a triangle, you lose. If they do form a triangle, then right triangles beat all other triangles and acute triangles beat obtuse triangles.

THE QUESTIONS

Suppose that we have 50 straws of lengths 1, 2, 3, . . ., 50. Playing the game above, I draw 3 straws.

1. How many different "hands" of straws can I draw?

2. How many different triangles can be formed?

3. How many of these triangles are—

 a) acute?

 b) obtuse?

 c) right triangles?

Suppose I play this game with 10 000 straws of lengths 1, 2, 3, . . ., 10 000.

4. What is the probability that I will lose on my first choice of 3 straws?

5. What is the probability that I will win if two of us can make triangles?

A BEGINNING

Let us look at the problem with 9 straws of length 1, 2, 3, . . ., 9. We shall list the possible hands of 3 straws—that is, the possible lengths of the 3 straws, with the shortest length first and the longest length last (see fig. 8.8).

123 124 125 126 127 128 129, 134 135 136 137 138 139, 145 146 147 148
  149, 156 157 158 159, 167 168 169, 178 179, 189
234 235 236 237 238 239, 245 246 247 248 249, 256 257 258 259,
  267 268 269, 278 279, 289
345 346 347 348 349, 356 357 358 359, 367 368 369, 378 379, 389
456 457 458 459, 467 468 469, 478 479, 489
567 568 569, 578 579, 589
678 679, 689
789

Fig. 8.8

There are eighty-four triples here; thirty-four can form triangles, and nine form acute triangles. The groups that can form triangles are underlined, the acute triangles are in boldface.

We can organize our data by listing in the following chart the number of triples that are associated with the shortest straw:

Length of straw	1	2	3	4	5	6	7	Total
Number of triples	28	21	15	10	6	3	1	84
Number of triangles	0	6	9	9	6	3	1	34
Number of acute triangles	0	0	0	2	3	3	1	9

There is one right triangle (345) and twenty-four obtuse triangles. The probability that the straws form a triangle is 34/84. If a triangle is formed, the probability that it is acute is 9/34.

54. Making Triangles out of Cardboard Strips

Here are two recipes for making triangles out of cardboard strips:

Recipe 1. Take a long narrow piece of cardboard, crease at two places, and fold gently at creases until a beautiful triangle is formed.

Recipe 2. Take a long narrow piece of cardboard, crease once, crease again on the longer of the two uncreased segments, then fold gently into a beautiful triangle.

Wait a second! I tried these recipes several times, and I didn't have much luck at all. What's going on?

THE QUESTIONS

Make your creases at places that are 1/100 of the way along the strip.

1. If you use recipe 1—

   a) how many different pairs of creases are possible?

   b) how many of these will form a triangle?

2. If you use recipe 2—

   a) how many different pairs of creases are possible?

   b) how many result in triangles?

The creases can be made anywhere along the strip.

3. What are the chances that you can form a triangle—

   a) using recipe 1?

   b) using recipe 2?

A BEGINNING

Let us assume that the strip is one unit long and the creases can be made only at places one-tenth unit apart, that is, 0.1, 0.2, 0.3, 0.4, 0.5, 0.6, 0.7, 0.8, and 0.9. First we try recipe 1. There are thirty-six different pairs of creases. Notice that we need not distinguish between creases at 0.1, 0.2 and 0.2, 0.1 because the result is the same. The different pairs are at 0.1, 0.2; 0.1, 0.3; . . .; 0.1, 0.9; 0.2, 0.3; . . .; 0.2, 0.9; . . .; and 0.8, 0.9. Of these possibilities, six yield triangles: 0.2, 0.6; 0.4, 0.6; 0.4, 0.8 (these three yield a 2-4-4-shaped triangle); 0.3, 0.6; 0.4, 0.7; 0.3, 0.7 (these three yield a 3-3-4-shaped triangle). So the probability is 1/6 that a triangle is formed.

For recipe 2 the situation is somewhat different because the order of the creases matters. Furthermore, if our first crease is at 0.5, we won't bother with another crease because there is no shorter segment. There are fifty-two different scenarios:

$$0.1, 0.2; \ldots; 0.1, 0.9$$
$$0.2, 0.3; \ldots; 0.2, 0.9$$
$$0.3, 0.4; \ldots; 0.3, 0.9$$
$$0.4, 0.5; \ldots; 0.4, 0.9$$

and their reverse creases:

$$0.6, 0.1; \ldots; 0.6, 0.5$$
$$0.7, 0.1; \ldots; 0.7, 0.6$$
$$0.8, 0.1; \ldots; 0.8, 0.7$$
$$0.9, 0.1; \ldots; 0.9, 0.8$$

This totals $8 + 7 + 6 + 5 + 5 + 6 + 7 + 8 = 52$. Twelve of these pairs of creases result in triangles, the six listed for recipe 1 along with their reverse creases: 0.6, 0.2; 0.6, 0.4; 0.8, 0.4; 0.6, 0.3; 0.7, 0.3; and 0.7, 0.4. So the probability is 3/13 that a triangle is formed. This is better than 1/6.

55. Bring Your Social Security Card

The University of Arizona baseball team has not been drawing in the fans the way they used to. The athletic department has decided to run a big promotion to attract more fans. When you enter the park, you register the last four digits of your Social Security number. During the seventh inning of the game, prizes will be awarded. If the registered numbers of two people match, then the lucky pair will each receive a free Big Gulp. If the numbers of three people match, then instead of the drinks, the lucky ones will each receive a free dinner at Olson's on Broadway. If four numbers match, instead of the lesser prizes, each of the lucky people will receive an all-expense-paid trip to Disneyland. If five people have matching numbers, each receives a one-year, full-tuition scholarship to the university. If six people match, each will receive season basketball tickets. The athletic department has hired me to advise them on the size of the prizes and the probabilities of winning so that they don't lose their shirts while trying to draw in fans.

THE QUESTIONS

The fan's thoughts

1. *a*) How big would the crowd have to be for me to have an even chance of winning a Big Gulp? A dinner?

b) There are 10 000 seats in Wildcat Field. If all seats are filled, what are my chances of winning something, anything will do?

2. How big would the crowd have to be for there to be an even chance that—

a) two people win a Big Gulp? four people? six people? eight people? ten people?

b) three people win a dinner? six people? nine people?

c) four people win a trip to Disneyland? eight people?

d) five people win a scholarship?

e) six people win a season ticket to the basketball games? (I thought there weren't any tickets available.)

The athletic department's thoughts

3. If, by some miracle, 10 000 people show up, what damage can we expect?

a) In particular, how many people will win something?

Of those who win something, how many will win—

b) a drink?

c) a dinner?

d) a trip?

e) a scholarship?

f) a season ticket?

4. How big would the crowd have to be so that half of them actually win some kind of prize?

A BEGINNING

We have a good beginning on this problem. This is the same as the birthday problem, and chapter 5 is devoted entirely to it. We hope that by couching the problem in terms of 10 000 possibilities (a power of 10) rather than 365, the answers will fit a recognizable pattern.

Most of the aspects of the problem are not easily approached with simple formulas. As with the birthday problem, the best way to approach the multiple matches and a desirable way to approach all the problems is by computer simulation.

To put your answers into perspective, you should also perform the same inquiry with the middle two numbers of your Social Security number (there are 100 possibilities here), and then carry it out again with the first six numbers of your Social Security number (there are 1 million different possibilities here). As for me, I will do the problem with 100 possibilities and will complete the rest when I get a faster computer.

56. How Many Small Numbers Make a Big Number?

The Archimedean principle tells us that no matter how small a quantity is, if you add it to itself enough times, you can make an arbitrarily large quantity. But after studying geometric series, we know that if you take different-sized small quantities and add them together, there is no guarantee that you can surpass even the number 1. For example, 1/2, 1/4, 1/8, . . ., $1/2^n$, . . . make up an infinite collection of numbers that added together do not surpass 1. What would happen if we randomly drew proper fractions from a large tub of proper fractions and added them together? Would the situation be more likely to follow the Archimedean principle or a geometric series? One thing is certain—I'll bet we could get past the number 1. In fact, common sense tells us that we have a fifty-fifty chance of reaching or surpassing 1 after two draws from the tub. That's a good start.

THE QUESTIONS

1. On average, how many one-digit numbers must be added together to make a two-digit number?

2. On average, how many—

   a) two-digit numbers must be added together to make a three-digit number?

   b) one-digit numbers must be added together to make a three-digit number?

3. On average, how many positive numbers less than 1 must be added together to make a number greater than or equal to 1?

4. On average, how many positive numbers less than 1 must be added together to make a number greater than or equal to—

   a) 2?

   b) 3?

   c) 10?

   d) 100?

   e) 1/2?

   f) 1/3?

   g) 1/10?

5. For what number N does it take, on average, the sum of two numbers less than 1 to equal or surpass N?

A BEGINNING

Let us look at the positive integers less than 5, that is, 1, 2, 3, and 4. Now let us see how many of these numbers, on average, must be added together to equal or surpass 5.

There are sixteen possible pairs of two numbers:

$$11, 12, 13, \underline{14}, 21, 22, \underline{23}, \underline{24},$$
$$31, \underline{32}, \underline{33}, \underline{34}, \underline{41}, \underline{42}, \underline{43}, \underline{44}$$

The underlined pairs sum to 5 or more. There are ten such pairs. So 10/16 of the time two addends suffice; 6/16 of the time more addends are needed. Of these other six instances, 11, 12, 13, 21, 22, and 31, the probabilities of making 5 or more with one more addend are, respectively, 2/4, 3/4, 4/4, 3/4, 4/4, and 4/4. This equals 20/4. So the probability that three addends, but not two addends, are sufficient to equal 5 or more is

$$(1/16)(20/4) = 20/64.$$

There are four remaining instances: 111, 112, 121, and 211. The probabilities that one more addend will put them over the top are, respectively, 3/4, 4/4, 4/4, and 4/4. This adds to 15/4. So the probability that it takes exactly four addends to equal or surpass 5 is

$$(1/64)\,(15/4) = 15/256.$$

The one remaining possibility is 11111, and the probability of that happening is 1/256.

We conclude that, on average, it takes

$$(10/16)2 + (20/64)3 + (15/256)4 + (4/1024)5 = 625/256,$$

or about 2.4414, numbers less than 5 to add up to 5 or more.

57. Conflict among the Natural Numbers

Some numbers get along better together than others. Those that have a lot in common are naturally more compatible. A measure of this compatibility between two numbers is their greatest common factor. For large numbers, finding the GCF of two numbers takes some effort, but it can be done by using the Euclidean algorithm. Here is how it works for the small numbers 6 and 10: (1) Divide 6 into 10 and note the remainder, 4. (2) Divide the remainder 4 into the divisor 6 and note the second remainder, 2. (3) Repeat this process: divide 2 into 4 and note the remainder, 0. The process stops with the remainder 0, and the GCF is the last divisor, 2. The number of steps in the algorithm in this particular example is 3. We call this the *conflict index* and label it with $C(n, m)$. Thus $C(10, 6) = 3$. The conflict quotient $C(N)$ of a number N is the average of the conflict indices of N with all smaller numbers K. Thus,

$$C(N) = (1/(N-1))(C(N, 1) + \ldots + C(N, N-1)).$$

The war quotient $W(N)$ for a population of the first N numbers is the average of all $C(M, K)$ for $N > M > K > 0$.

This problem examines how conflicts increase as the population grows.

THE QUESTIONS

The population is growing from 1 to 10 000.

1. Which two numbers have the highest conflict index?

When the conflict index reaches 10, tempers begin to flare. In particular, a fight breaks out between the first pair of numbers with index 10; another breaks out with the first pair that reaches 11. Fights continue like this until the conflict reaches 40. At that point a murder takes place (the larger number killing the smaller one).

2. *a*) How many fights break out, and who is involved?

b) Do any murders take place?

c) Predict how big the population would have to be for a murder to take place.

An *irascible* number is a number whose conflict quotient exceeds that of all lesser numbers. A *peaceable* number is a number that has a smaller quotient than that of any larger number.

3. *a*) Find the largest irascible number. What is its quotient?

b) Find the largest peaceable number. What is its quotient?

When the conflict quotient reaches 5, the number becomes a problem to society. The first irascible that exceeds 5 is put in jail. The same goes for the first that exceeds 6, and so on, until the quotient reaches 10. If the conflict quotient exceeds 10, the number is put in a maximum-security prison.

4. *a*) How many irascible numbers go to jail, and who are they?

b) Approximately how big would the population have to be to produce a misanthrope that must go to prison?

When a quotient of a peaceable number first reaches at least 5, the number receives a peace prize. The first ones to reach 6, 7, 8, and 9 also achieve this distinction. The first peaceable number with a quotient surpassing 10 becomes a saint.

5. *a*) How many receive the peace prize, and to whom is it awarded?

b) Is anyone bestowed sainthood? If not, approximately how big would the population have to be to produce a saint?

Skirmishes break out every time the war quotient passes an integer. They get more serious, until a war breaks out when the quotient passes 10. War occurs again when the quotient surpasses 11, then 12, and so on up to 20. Annihilation occurs when the quotient surpasses 20.

6. *a*) As the population grows to 10 000, how many skirmishes break out?

b) Approximately how big would the population have to be for total destruction to occur?

A BEGINNING

Suppose the population grows from 1 to 6. The following is a list of all conflict indices:

$C(2, 1) = 1$	$C(5, 1) = 1$
$C(3, 1) = 1$	$C(5, 2) = 2$
$C(3, 2) = 2$	$C(5, 3) = 3$
$C(4, 1) = 1$	$C(5, 4) = 2$
$C(4, 2) = 1$	$C(6, 1) = C(6, 2) = C(6, 3) = 1$
$C(4, 3) = 2$	$C(6, 4) = C(6, 5) = 2$

Note:

$C(2) = 1$	$W(2) = 1$
$C(3) = 1.5$	$W(3) = 1.33$
$C(4) = 1.33$	$W(4) = 1.33$
$C(5) = 2$	$W(5) = 1.6$
$C(6) = 1.4$	$W(6) = 1.533$

In this population, 2 and 4 are peaceable numbers; 3 and 5 are irascible numbers.

A skirmish breaks out when 3 joins the population because $W(3) > 1$ and $W(2) \not> 1$.

58. Earthquakes on the Real Line

It is well known that periodically the open interval $(0, 1)$ on the real line is rocked by major earthquakes. The quakes are composed of a series of tremors, all of equal strength. There may be a million or more tremors in a single quake. A tremor can be thought of as a function on the interval of the form $A(x - x^2)$. A is a positive real number, and it measures the intensity of the quake, the way the Richter scale does. Since the points are displaced internally within the interval, it follows (you can figure this one out) that the intensity of the quake must be greater than 1 and less than 4. Each real number in $(0, 1)$ is affected by each tremor—some being perennially displaced throughout the quake, some staying put, but most being inexorably driven to specified deposit sites. A good way to analyze a quake is to examine its aftermath.

THE QUESTIONS

1. If after the quake, all points in the interval $(0, 1)$ are found congregated at the point 0.4—

   a) what was the intensity of the quake?

   b) how many tremors must have occurred during the quake?

2. What is the intensity of the strongest quake that eventually leaves all the points in the interval deposited at a single site?

3. If the intensity of the quake is 3.5—

   a) what single point stays fixed throughout the whole quake?

   b) what two points alternate positions throughout the whole quake?

   c) what is the fate of most of the points?

4. What range(s) on the Richter scale is (are) indicative of a quake that deposits points at—

   a) two distinct sites?

   b) four distinct sites?

5. Comment on the following theories about earthquakes:

   a) If the intensity of two earthquakes is nearly identical, then the results (number and placement of deposit sites) are nearly identical.

   b) Neighboring points are driven to the same deposit site.

   c) The stronger the earthquake is, the more deposit sites there are.

   d) The more deposit sites there are, the rarer the quake is.

   e) There are earthquakes that have any number of deposit sites—3, 4, 5, 6, 7, 8, 9, 10, and so on.

A BEGINNING

Suppose that we have a quake of intensity 1.75. The quake function is $1.75(x - x^2)$. If we follow the relocations of the point 0.5, we find that successive tremors send it to 0.4375, 0.4306640, 0.4290869, 0.4286998, 0.4286035, 0.4285794, 0.4285734, 0.4285719, 0.4285716, 0.4285715, 0.4285714, 0.4285714.

So from the seven-place accuracy of our readout, it looks as if 0.5 has permanently relocated to the site 0.4285714. It reached this location after eleven tremors. Now admittedly, the point may still be moving slightly during succeeding tremors. Using double precision, we can get our decimals to sixteen-place accuracy and find out what further movement takes place. Doing this, we find that the point continues to move through fourteen more tremors, and after twenty-five tremors, it settles at the site 0.4285714285714286. This is the best we can do with our BASIC program. We recognize this site as 3/7. It turns out that all points between 0 and 1 eventually relocate at the single site, 3/7. The chart in figure 8.9 shows the time it takes some particular points to relocate to 0.4285714.

Point	Number of tremors
0.5	11
0.4 or 0.6	11
0.3 or 0.7	12
0.2 or 0.8	13
0.1 or 0.9	15
0.0000001 or 0.9999999	39

Fig. 8.9

Notice that the points x and $1 - x$ that we chose are relocated in exactly the same way by the quake function. Although we didn't choose 3/7, it is easily shown that 3/7 never moves from its home, and 4/7 moves in with 3/7 after one tremor. Notice also that the limiting feature of seven-place accuracy allows us to use only the 9 999 999 real numbers from 0.0000001 to 0.9999999 in our analysis of the quake.

This analysis indicates (assuming seven-place accuracy) that if the Richter scale shows 1.75, the points are all deposited at the single site 0.4285714 (or 3/7) and the quake lasts a minimum of thirty-nine tremors.

59. A Hailstorm Strikes the Natural Numbers

The life of a natural number can have its ups and downs. If you don't believe it, just ask one who has lived through a hailstorm. This particular storm tosses the numbers about in the following way: if N is even, it drops to $N/2$; if N is odd, it is lifted to $(3N + 1)/2$. The choppy ride continues like this forever unless the number 1 is reached; 1 is the ground. Some numbers fall to the ground immediately; others are buffeted all over the place. For example, 8 falls to 4, then to 2, and then to the ground. In contrast, 13 takes quite a ride:

$$13 \to 20 \to 10 \to 5 \to 8 \to 4 \to 2 \to 1$$

We say that 8 has a trip of length 3; 13 has a trip of length 7. The number 8 did not exceed its original height, whereas 13 reached an altitude of 20.

THE QUESTIONS

During this hailstorm, N is $\leq 10\ 000$:

1. Which number reaches the highest altitude, and what is this record height?

2. Which number experiences the longest trip, and how long is it?

3. Which number experiences the greatest airsickness?

4. Which number experiences the most consecutive—

   a) downdrafts? How many are there?

   b) updrafts? How many are there?

Find the first (smallest) number to break the following coveted marks:

5. *a)* Reaches an altitude of at least 1 million

   b) Takes a trip of length at least 1 thousand

   c) Experiences at least ten consecutive updrafts

6. Comment about the following theories concerning hailstorms:

   a) No number N larger than 100 rises above N^2.

   b) No number can stay above its own altitude more than 90 percent of its trip.

   c) There is no longest trip.

   d) There is no maximum airsickness quotient.

   e) Many neighboring numbers experience trips of the same length (though not necessarily the same scenery). In fact, there is no upper limit on the number of consecutive numbers that can experience the same length trip.

d) Given any sequence of ups and downs, there is a number that begins its ride in this fashion. In particular, some numbers begin their ride with an arbitrarily long string of consecutive updrafts.

e) All numbers eventually hit the ground.

A BEGINNING

The chart in figure 8.10 show the trips of the numbers less than 10.

Trip	Length of trip	Maximum altitude	Airsickness quotient
$2 \to 1$	1	2	1
$3 \to 5 \to 8 \to 4 \to 2 \to 1$	5	8	2.67
$4 \to 2 \to 1$	2	4	1
$5 \to 8 \to 4 \to 2 \to 1$	4	8	1.6
$6 \to 3 \to 5 \to 8 \to 4 \to 2 \to 1$	6	8	1.33
$7 \to 11 \to 17 \to 26 \to 13 \to 20 \to$ $\quad 10 \to 5 \to 8 \to 4 \to 2 \to 1$	11	26	3.71
$8 \to 4 \to 2 \to 1$	3	8	1
$9 \to 14 \to 7 \to 11 \to 17 \to 26 \to$ $\quad 13 \to 20 \to 10 \to 5 \to 8 \to 4 \to 2 \to 1$	13	26	2.89

Fig. 8.10

In this group, 9 had the longest trip, 7 and 9 tied for the highest altitude achieved, and 7 experienced the worst case of airsickness. The airsickness quotient is the maximum altitude attained divided by the number itself. Numbers tend to get quite ill when raised to altitudes well beyond what they are used to. The record for the most consecutive downdrafts was three, and it was, not surprisingly, recorded by 8. The record for the most consecutive updrafts was also three, and it was recorded by 7 and duplicated by 9 when 9 was caught in 7's updraft. Notice that the trips are often identical at the end because a number gets caught in the updraft of another number and is carried along on the same trip.

60. The Battle of Trafalgar

On 21 October 1805, a British fleet of twenty-seven warships under the command of Lord Nelson met a combined French and Spanish fleet of thirty-three ships and captured twenty ships without a loss. This was known as the battle of Trafalgar, and it was a decisive naval battle of the Napoleonic Wars. It is acknowledged that it was Nelson's unorthodox strategy that won the day.

Naturally, if the numbers are the only determining factor, the larger fleet should eventually win the battle. More precisely, if the first skirmish results in the loss of a single ship, the probability of that ship belonging to a particular fleet should be directly proportional to the sizes of the fleets.

Using only the numbers, we shall try to model a strategy that might explain what Nelson did. We shall split the Nelson fleet into two different groups and have them, in turn, force a split in the combined Spanish and French fleets, forming two groups. The groups will face off in separate battles. The survivors of the two battles then compete in a final battle.

THE QUESTIONS

1. If Nelson had not used any strategy and the two sides had fought until one side was defeated—

   a) what is the probability that the French and Spanish side would have won?

   b) assuming that the French and Spanish side won, how many ships of theirs would survive?

2. How did Nelson divide his fleet so that he not only won but had the greatest possible number of surviving ships? How many ships could survive under this scheme?

A BEGINNING

Suppose that side A has 5 ships and side B has 3. Suppose that the battle proceeds as a sequence of skirmishes; each skirmish results in the loss of one ship. The probability that a side loses a ship is directly dependent on the relative numbers in the battle.

For example, in the first skirmish, A has 5 ships and B has 3, so there are 8 ships in all. We can expect A to win 5/8 of the time and B to win 3/8 of the time. In the second skirmish we have two possibilities. If A won the first skirmish, it has 5 ships and B has 2; so the chances for it to win again are 5/7. If A lost the first skirmish, it has 4 ships, and B has 3; so the chances for it to win this skirmish are 4/7. As we proceed to check the possibilities, the probabilities get complicated quickly. The diagram in figure 8.11 helps put the process into understandable terms.

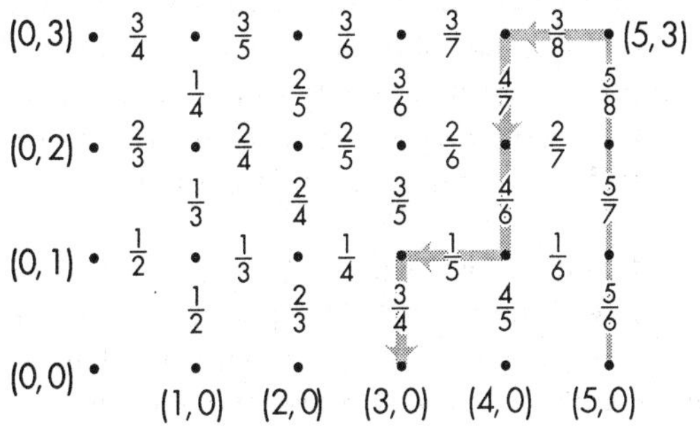

Fig. 8.11

We notice that if side A wins every skirmish, then the battle is over in three skirmishes and all 5 of A's ships survive. The probability of that is $(5/8) (5/7) (5/6) = 125/336$. Another possibility has been drawn on the diagram. In this scenario the winners, in succession, are B, A, A, B, A. This scenario takes five skirmishes and leaves A with 3 survivors. The probability of this happening is

$$\frac{3}{8} \cdot \frac{4}{7} \cdot \frac{4}{6} \cdot \frac{1}{5} \cdot \frac{3}{4}.$$

Table 8.3 shows all the probabilities, assuming A is the winner.

It is possible that B will win the battle. The probabilities that B wins and leaves survivors are—

3 survivors: $\dfrac{1458}{40320}$; 2 survivors: $\dfrac{1892}{40320}$; 1 survivor: $\dfrac{1191}{40320}$.

This can be verified by following the probability paths of figure 8.11 to the points $(0, 3)$, $(0, 2)$, and $(0, 1)$.

Out of the 40 320 possible outcomes, 35 779 of them leave A as the winner. That is 88.74 percent. If we assume that A is the winner, then out of those 35 729 scenarios we can expect 5 survivors 15 000 times, 4 survivors 10 848 times, 3 survivors 5868 times, 2 survivors 2872 times, and 1 survivor 1241 times. The average number or expected number of survivors is 4.0018, that is, 4.

Now let us see how some strategy can pay off. Suppose that side A and side B both have 6 ships. Side A could adopt the following strategy: Have 1 of its ships split off 3 of B's ships and engage them in battle. At the same time, 5 of A's ships battle 3 of B's ships. In the second battle, as we have

Table 8.3
Probabilities If A *Wins*

Number of survivors		Probability
5	$\dfrac{5}{8} \cdot \dfrac{5}{7} \cdot \dfrac{5}{6}$	$\dfrac{125}{336}$
4	$\dfrac{5}{8} \cdot \dfrac{5}{7} \cdot \dfrac{1}{6} \cdot \dfrac{4}{5} + \dfrac{5}{8} \cdot \dfrac{2}{7} \cdot \dfrac{4}{6} \cdot \dfrac{4}{5}$ $+ \dfrac{3}{8} \cdot \dfrac{4}{7} \cdot \dfrac{4}{6} \cdot \dfrac{4}{5}$	$\dfrac{452}{1680}$
3	$\dfrac{5}{8} \cdot \dfrac{5}{7} \cdot \dfrac{1}{6} \cdot \dfrac{1}{5} \cdot \dfrac{3}{4} + \dfrac{5}{8} \cdot \dfrac{2}{7} \cdot \dfrac{4}{6} \cdot \dfrac{1}{5} \cdot \dfrac{3}{4}$ $+ \dfrac{5}{8} \cdot \dfrac{2}{7} \cdot \dfrac{2}{6} \cdot \dfrac{3}{5} \cdot \dfrac{3}{4}$ $+ \dfrac{3}{8} \cdot \dfrac{4}{7} \cdot \dfrac{4}{6} \cdot \dfrac{1}{5} \cdot \dfrac{3}{4}$ $+ \dfrac{3}{8} \cdot \dfrac{4}{7} \cdot \dfrac{2}{6} \cdot \dfrac{3}{5} \cdot \dfrac{3}{4}$ $+ \dfrac{3}{8} \cdot \dfrac{3}{7} \cdot \dfrac{3}{6} \cdot \dfrac{3}{5} \cdot \dfrac{3}{4}$	$\dfrac{978}{6720}$
2	The numerators of the ten respective addends are $5 \cdot 5 \cdot 1 \cdot 1 \cdot 1 \cdot 2$, $5 \cdot 2 \cdot 4 \cdot 1 \cdot 1 \cdot 2$, $5 \cdot 2 \cdot 2 \cdot 3 \cdot 1 \cdot 2$, $5 \cdot 2 \cdot 2 \cdot 2 \cdot 2 \cdot 2$, $3 \cdot 4 \cdot 4 \cdot 1 \cdot 1 \cdot 2$, $3 \cdot 4 \cdot 2 \cdot 3 \cdot 1 \cdot 2$, $3 \cdot 4 \cdot 2 \cdot 2 \cdot 2 \cdot 2$, $3 \cdot 3 \cdot 3 \cdot 3 \cdot 1 \cdot 2$, $3 \cdot 3 \cdot 3 \cdot 2 \cdot 2 \cdot 2$, and $3 \cdot 3 \cdot 3 \cdot 2 \cdot 2 \cdot 2$. The denominator is always $8 \cdot 7 \cdot 6 \cdot 5 \cdot 4 \cdot 3$.	$\dfrac{1436}{20160}$
1	There are fifteen different scenarios to sum. The answer is at the right.	$\dfrac{1191}{40320}$

just discovered, A almost surely wins, and if it does, it can expect 4 survivors. In the first battle, B will almost surely win and most likely will have all 3 ships survive. So the final battle between sides pits the 4 survivors of A against the 3 of B. A can expect to win and have survivors, too. Try it.

Of course it is a big assumption that one ship can occupy three other ships long enough for another battle involving eight ships to play itself out. Because this is mathematics, not war, we can make such assumptions.

APPENDIX

Problem solving is an art that is not satisfactorily understood. Almost every expert would agree, however, that the more mathematical tools the students have to work with, the better problem solvers they will become. The challenge for the problem solver is to pick the right mix of tools. Mathematics courses tend to present the different areas of study as separate and distinct from each other. This is a mistake. Algebra, geometry, and probability, for example, have an enormous overlap. I believe that if students could spend more time in this overlap, they would gain a greater understanding and appreciation of mathematics. The good problem solvers are the ones who can integrate their understanding of these separate subjects and thereby experience the synergism that lies at the heart of the creative process.

The matrix below relates the exploratory problems of this book to the subject matter of courses taught. This is meant to be an aid to students and teachers, and it can be helpful if it is understood in the context of the opening paragraph. An "X" in the space simply means that the content of the course may bear on certain approaches to solving the problem. It is entirely possible that a successful approach will not rely on material from the marked courses. This is especially true for the number theory and calculus designations. A mark in the "N" column simply means that elementary properties of natural numbers are involved. It does not mean that the material from an upper-level college course on number theory is assumed. A mark in the "C" column means that a general solution might be facilitated with a knowledge of calculus. It does NOT mean that calculus is a prerequisite. I must emphasize again that a student who has not had the courses indicated should not be deterred from experimenting and exploring.

EXPLORATORY PROBLEMS IN MATHEMATICS

Key: A, algebra; G, geometry; N, number theory; F, finite mathematics; P, probability; C, calculus

Problem Number	A	G	N	F	P	C
1		X	X			
2	X		X			
3			X			
4	X		X			
5	X	X				
6	X	X				
7						
8	X		X			
9			X			
10	X		X			
11		X	X			
12		X	X			
13	X	X		X		
14	X		X			
15		X	X			
16	X	X	X			
17	X		X			
18	X				X	X
19	X				X	
20	X	X	X			
21	X		X			
22	X	X	X			
23	X	X	X			
24	X				X	X	X
25	X	X				
26	X	X				
27		X	X			
28	X	X		X		
29	X	X				
30	X	X	X			

Problem Number	A	G	N	F	P	C
31	X	X	X			
32		X	X			
33	X			X		
34	X		X			
35	X	X	X			
36	X	X	X			
37		X	X			
38	X				X	X
39			X	X		
40			X			
41	X					X
42		X				
43	X		X			
44	X		X			
45	X				X	
46	X			X	X	X
47	X				X	X
48	X	X	X			
49	X		X			
50	X	X				X
51	X		X			X
52	X		X			X
53	X			X	X	
54	X			X	X	X
55	X			X	X	
56	X			X	X	
57	X	X				
58	X					
59	X					
60	X	X		X	X	X